Jessica has written such a marvelous book about t... As Jessica weaves her story with the story of Ruth and Naomi, you will find yourself laughing and crying. It is a story of belonging and remaining steadfast in some of life's hardships with the beautiful reminder you are never alone. This is a must-read for every military family and those who want to know more about their journeys.

AARON LYNN, Lead Pastor of Naples First Church of the Nazarene

Never Alone will help military and nonmilitary spouses alike understand how to struggle well in life's challenges, how to stand in the strength of their convictions, and how to live a life filled with love and beauty before God. As a seasoned military spouse, Manfre captures the essence of Ruth's conviction and gives us a language to speak amidst an ever-changing landscape. *Never Alone* is a clarion call for all spouses who find themselves weary in well-doing, where the changes and chances of this life are hard to bear, but who know that this journey is never meant to be traversed alone.

JAMAL SCARLETT, United States Navy Chaplain

Navigating life as a military spouse is harder than it looks, filled with moments of deep loneliness and overwhelming hardship. Yet many are still carrying that weight alone. Enter Jessica, the neighbor and best friend that every military spouse needs in their back pocket who also just happens to know exactly what you need to hear right when you need to hear it. Ultimately, she reminds every reader that there is a God who is just as present for you today as He was for Ruth yesterday.

CORIE WEATHERS, Licensed Professional Counselor (LPC) and Army chaplain spouse

We all experience moments in life when we feel no one understands, and that's a lonely place. Jessica's book, *Never Alone,* can make you feel as though she's peering into your heart and soul. I love Jessica's courage in sharing her heart and confidence in God's infinite love that shines through her work.

KRISTA SIMPSON ANDERSON, Gold Star spouse, 2018 Armed Forces Insurance Military Spouse of the Year, and cofounder of The Unquiet Professional

A gripping firsthand look into the behind the scenes world of a military spouse. The lessons in *Never Alone* provide multi-tool for those on the journey of faith and service. Finally, a recognition of military spouses and the true cost of supporting those who wear the uniform.

ADAM CHASE MILLSAP, Marine and Green Beret veteran; award-winning filmmaker and producer

Jessica Manfre delivers an honest and nuanced road map for how to succeed as a military spouse. Not only does *Never Alone* deliver raw personal stories from Manfre, it also discusses the challenges of military spouses from a scientific and spiritual perspective. A must-read for any military spouse, and an important read for any service member wanting to understand how their better half copes with their absence.

NICK PALMISCIANO, *New York Times* bestselling author and Army combat veteran

As a military spouse of seventeen years, I found it refreshing to read this book and realize how Ruth's story is so relatable to the military spouse. I cried, I laughed, and I sighed as I read through the pages of *Never Alone*. You will finish the book with a newfound strength and understanding that you truly are never alone and God is with you always.

BRITTANY BOCCHER, 2017 Armed Forces Insurance Military Spouse of the Year and founder of Discovering Your Spark

Faith is revealed to us through powerful storytelling. A burning bush. A sea parted. A force darker than evil and a God full of mercy and light. These stories give us more than lessons; they give us hope. Jessica Manfre is a master storyteller. *Never Alone* weaves together the beautiful triumphant heart of Ruth with the unwavering strength of military spouses. It's a story of faith, friendship, service, and most of all, love. A must-read for every military spouse.

TESSA ROBINSON, Editor in Chief for We Are The Mighty; former CIA agent

As an Army special forces veteran, my mind was always on the next mission while everything at home seemed secondary. The world needs to know our military spouses are the true foundation for ensuring force readiness. Without our spouses and families securing the home front, we couldn't do what we do. *Never Alone* is a loud reminder of the price our families pay so we can serve. It's also a deep calling into the faith that sustains us as we navigate the realities of military life from those waiting at home to the warriors on the battlefields across the globe. Jessica takes you on an extraordinary journey through this book by giving readers the truth about the toll loneliness can take while simultaneously reinforcing our faith in God walking with us through it all.

TRAVIS WILSON, CEO of Alpha Elite Performance, president of Alpha Elite Performance Outdoors, and retired Army Green Beret

In the eighteen years I have been a military spouse, I have been on the brink of feeling broken more than a couple of times. As a physician's assistant, I've seen the results of the negative impact loneliness can have on the body and the mind. Jessica Manfre has crafted into the printed word the message that my soul has spoken in my quiet prayers. This is a stunning piece of work, one that will have well-loved dog-eared pages as I continue to reference my favorite passages. Manfre has crafted a message of hope and inspiration that our journey is never a solitary one.

SAMANTHA GOMOLKA, PA-C, physician's assistant, Green Beret spouse, and Vice President of Development for Project 33 Memorial Foundation

RUTH, THE
MODERN
MILITARY
SPOUSE,
AND THE GOD
WHO GOES
WITH US

NEVER ALONE

JESSICA MANFRE, LMSW

MOODY PUBLISHERS
CHICAGO

Published in association with The Linda S. Glaz Literary Agency, 51670 Washington St., New Baltimore, MI 48047.

Emphasis to Scripture has been added by the author.

Edited by Pamela Joy Pugh and Megan B. Brown
Interior design: Brandi Davis
Cover design: Erik M. Peterson
Cover illustration of couple praying copyright © 2022 by Prixel Creative / Lightstock (222966). All rights reserved.
Cover illustration of wheat field © 2022 by Valentina Rusinova / Shutterstock (94975135). All rights reserved.
Author photo: Ian Herbst

Library of Congress Cataloging-in-Publication Data

Names: Manfre, Jessica, author.
Title: Never alone : Ruth, the modern military spouse, and the God who goes with us / Jessica Manfre.
Description: Chicago : Moody Publishers, 2022. | Includes bibliographical references. | Summary: "In the book of Ruth, we witness a woman's journey of loss, loyalty, and love. Sound familiar? These are hallmarks of the military life. Our lives are fraught with heartache and sacrifice. But even when we're in a faraway, foreign land, He is not lost and has not lost us"-- Provided by publisher.
Identifiers: LCCN 2022033311 (print) | LCCN 2022033312 (ebook) | ISBN 9780802428400 | ISBN 9780802475565 (ebook)
Subjects: LCSH: Bible. Ruth--Criticism, interpretation, etc. | Military spouses--Religious life.
Classification: LCC BS1315.52 .M29 2022 (print) | LCC BS1315.52 (ebook) | DDC 222/.3506--dc23/eng/20221024
LC record available at https://lccn.loc.gov/2022033311
LC ebook record available at https://lccn.loc.gov/2022033312

Websites referenced were accurate at the time of the original publication but may have since changed or ceased to exist. The inclusion of website references does not imply publisher endorsement of the site's entire contents.

Originally delivered by fleets of horse-drawn wagons, the affordable paperbacks from D. L. Moody's publishing house resourced the church and served everyday people. Now, after more than 125 years of publishing and ministry, Moody Publishers' mission remains the same—even if our delivery systems have changed a bit. For more information on other books (and resources) created from a biblical perspective, go to www.moodypublishers.com or write to:

Moody Publishers
820 N. LaSalle Boulevard
Chicago, IL 60610

1 3 5 7 9 10 8 6 4 2

Printed in the United States of America

For all the little boys and girls who grew up like me, with their noses buried in books, dreaming about writing their hearts out one day. I see you.

CONTENTS

LET'S TALK
ABOUT IT

One early morning I found myself blissfully alone with my coffee, unapologetically hiding from my children as the sun was just starting to sparkle and shine through my living room window. While enjoying the beautiful moments of coveted silence and coffee sipping—I grabbed my Bible.

Ruth and Naomi's story had always been one of my favorites, which is probably why my fingers easily turned to their pages. There I sat, breathing the book of Ruth deep into my soul while simultaneously allowing the coffee to wake up my brain. As I began journeying with these women to Bethlehem, I had an epiphany.

Their story was so much *more* than I ever fathomed. How had I missed it all this time? My eyes saw those small words on their pages for what felt like the first time. My heart—or possibly God Himself—seemed to be saying: God's Word has a message beautifully woven, even for military spouses. Even for me.

The story of Ruth comes to us in the Old Testament in a time when the judges were ruling, as the nation did not yet have a king. Over these four hundred or so years, some of the judges were more influential for the Lord than others. On the whole, it was an era of the people rebelling against God, suffering the consequences, repenting, being restored, and starting the cycle all over again. Picture a hamster wheel of shenanigans.

The Jewish people were scurrying around like blind mice in the dark but doing bad stuff while they did it. Rather than following God, people did what was right in their own eyes (Judges 17:6).

Basically, it was like the Wild, Wild West, y'all.

This was a desperate time, filled with loss and rife with the disappointment of our God as He watched the unrest and ugly sin from above. Add a famine to all the fun and we've got a pretty terrible time. "Hangry" and hard knocks don't mix well.

The book of Ruth begins with Naomi following her husband, Elimelech, to a new land, a pagan one. Considering famine was often, though not always, a punishment from God, running away from it was probably a horrible idea on his part. He should have stayed and trusted God to provide. Just saying.

They fled their homeland and replanted roots in a place without their community of faith or support of any kind. Sound familiar?

I am one of those people who is absolutely obsessed with reading good books. One of the reasons I adored Ruth initially was its rich narration. When I'm reading, I want to feel the words and actually see it all play out in my head. Walking through Ruth, I could see it all so clearly. Although the author of this book is never named, tradition points to Samuel.[1]

Hats off to you, sir, for creating a masterpiece.

Ruth and Naomi light something up inside me. One of the things I believe our world is missing is *kindness*. Lovingkindness, to be exact. Considering what was going on way back then, I think I am safe in assuming it was more than lacking then. Despite this, we are privy to lovingkindness in action through Ruth.

The continuous theme of her story showcases loss, loneliness, loyalty, lovingkindness, *and* a beautiful unwavering faith, which are hallmark and ever-present emotions for military spouses everywhere. Where would we be without these to hold on to? When I recognized that our journey in this military life was so familiar to Ruth's and Naomi's throughout the book, the hair on my arms stood up—and it wasn't the caffeine hitting my bloodstream, I promise!

Within that moment, I closed my eyes and placed myself in both Moab and Bethlehem so many generations before, alone and scared. Those feelings so achingly matched my own life as a brand-new military spouse that I could feel that weight of loneliness, an unmissed old friend, trying to drown me once again.

Military spouses are often told that we *knew* what we signed up for. But that's an underinformed statement. It doesn't matter how many seasoned spouses share their experiences with you prior to your own military marriage or what you research to steel yourself for what's coming—you'll never know how deeply the military life will impact you until you start wading through it.

And wade—barely above water—you will.

As a licensed social worker and therapist, I *know* the clinical and mental health impacts of that weight you are carrying. On a personal level, I ache with you. Even with my educational and professional background to support myself, I've been in the pit of loneliness more than once. But I crawled my way out, changed but not broken. I promise, you can too. But first, you absolutely must process and understand loneliness.

Through this book, I want to help you unpack it all.

No one mentions the way your heart will ache in devastation when you find yourself far from your loved ones or *any* familiar support. Instead, you've heard about the adventure of exploring the world as you move continually. People definitely don't discuss the implications on the military marriage when loss and isolation are fueling everything, instead of what should be love leading the way. Let's also not forget church hunting in finding that spiritual home. Despite the scary and lonesome life, we charge on in faith and hope. Military spouses are just like Ruth in so many ways.

Ruth's own words of "where you go I will go" are shockingly powerful in demonstrating the devotion and love she had for Naomi. Despite the overwhelming challenge of leaving her home, she swore an oath to Naomi and stood in the strength of her conviction, despite the circumstances.

Any of this ringing a bell?

We military spouses tend to desperately cleave to our service-member just as Ruth did with Naomi. But unlike the continuous physical connection they shared, we suffer through long separations as we navigate unknown spaces time and again, seemingly alone. This tends to be where hopelessness and deep loneliness begin to settle like lead, causing an unmovable weight of despair.

Loneliness can eat away at you, festering in your heart if you let it.

To my sweet friends who found this book and aren't military or veteran spouses, I'm talking to you too. I pray the words I write call to your hearts and make you see your military community members in a different light. And if you, too, are going through a lonely season, well, grab on to me, friend. I'm here for you too!

We are in this shared, beautiful and challenging life together. I firmly believe that we desperately need one another in order to *struggle well*. It's the way we'll grow, just as Ruth and Naomi did.

As Ruth brings us through foreign lands filled with hardship and uncertainty, we'll witness the beauty of hope and faith being restored. Ruth's story will also demonstrate lovingkindness in action, a character trait we should all aspire to.

Friend, I am so glad you are here! We only learn and grow when we make ourselves uncomfortable. As human beings we strive to feel good, right? It's only natural to feel a nervousness when you embark on an unknown path or try something new. Your brain is trying to protect you, but in this case, it hinders you. Don't let it.

A close friend and fellow therapist shared something a while back that resonated with me deeply—secrets make you sick. So, say it with me: no more hiding pain. Loneliness isn't a topic often discussed out in the open. We are going to change that.

1

LONELY HURTS

I f you are looking for inspiring words about focusing on the coming rainbow after hardship, this isn't that kind of chapter, at least not initially. We have some hard things to get through first, friend.

We are going to get right into the thick of being uncomfortable, opening up our hearts to our struggles. Why?

It's the only way to make it to the other side.

This is the side where hope and goodness reign supreme. Before you can have the bright and pretty of the rainbow you are so unapologetically anticipating, it's important to sit in and work *through* the dark to get there. And loneliness *is* dark. It's an ugly and uncomfortable feeling that can bring on the deepest of despair and unbearable heartache. Staying in that space is painful, but without processing the "why" of it, you can't move forward *through* it.

I, too, have battled with loneliness and looked for ways to understand it.

As I was writing this book, I knew I'd be sharing the stories of my own military spouse journey and life lessons. But I had no idea I'd be unpacking my own loneliness trauma, with its roots going back to my three-year-old self.

My early years weren't picture perfect, despite being surrounded by a loving and very loud Italian family. Though my mother tried desperately to shield both my sister and me from our father's battle with alcoholism, there was no escaping it. I have cloudy memories of those years and of him, but the first one I can recall is visiting him while he was in drug and alcohol rehab.

I can still see the bunkhouse and feel him hugging me, his hands sweaty from nervousness and withdrawal.

When I was small, all I wanted to watch was *The Wizard of Oz*. Every night without fail, my mom would put it on after my bath. It's how I fell asleep, and I picked right back up the following night, like clockwork. My second memory of my father was of him fighting with my mother. Though I didn't know it then, he was drunk and apparently highly upset that I was hogging the television with my beloved movie.

I remember my mom carrying me from room to room, trying to get away from his loud and inebriated yelling. But I heard it—and vividly remember it all. Just like I remember the rain outside the moving trucks when we said goodbye to him not long after. My mother loved him with every breath she had—rehab to rehab she tried to save him from alcohol, and from himself. But the day he told her he didn't love her anymore, she just couldn't continue.

I don't blame her.

He'd go on to make some truly terrible choices that would land him in prison and gone from our lives for a long period of time. Though he came back into my life briefly when I was six, he disappeared shortly after. The state of Florida couldn't find him, and

> **Childhood loneliness can impact your life, even without your realizing it.**

I wouldn't hear from him again for almost a decade, until he surprised my sister and me with birthday cards when I was in high school.

To paint the full picture for you, he was *still* paying child support for me after I was married and had given birth to my first child at twenty-five.

I share this portion of my life not to evoke your sympathy for that little girl, but rather to demonstrate how deeply childhood loneliness can impact your life, even without your realizing it. From the outside looking in, I should have been fine without my father. My sister and I were raised by a strong mother, grandparents, aunts, a plethora of cousins, and actually lived in a loving home with my uncle, who treated us as if we were his own. I had father figures and many good things.

But I was still feeling lonely.

I ached for him, even though I didn't really know him. It would take me years to work through the issues his absence created in me.

When I was completing my master's program, part of my clinical requirements was to attend meetings for family members of alcoholics as well as the traditional Alcoholics Anonymous gatherings.

Within thirty minutes of my first meeting, I forgave him.

My work through my graduate studies gave me the tools I needed to understand who he was and work through his life choices to a place of empathy and true understanding. But it was also my own journey of faith that would light the way to actual forgiveness. It's a powerful thing. I absolutely love the Scripture about it, which says: "Be kind to one another, tenderhearted, forgiving one another, as God in Christ forgave you" (Ephesians 4:32).

It was so easy and clear. I got it. As an adult, I'd sure made my share of mistakes and transgressions. Who was I to hold on to his, like stones? Grace would lead me. In fact, I reached out to him right then and there. I told him I knew he had tried but ultimately couldn't work through his own demons to make it back to me before I was too old to keep waiting for him. But I said that it was okay and I was okay, and that he could rest knowing I wasn't holding on to his failings.

His wife would tell me later he cried and prayed his thanks out loud.

My heart no longer hurt from the loneliness of him walking away. As an adult I could examine the broken pieces of his life and see how his story unraveled the way it did. He was a baby boy born to a family who couldn't afford him and essentially didn't want him. His biological father also accused his mother of having an affair, denying his paternity. He was adopted by his maternal aunt, also an alcoholic. The name he'd lived with for three years was changed, and the siblings he'd been raised with were told he was no longer their brother. It wasn't a kind home and my heart aches for that little boy.

Though my mother was a stabilizing force in his life, he was only nineteen when they married and just twenty-one when I was born. A young man with unprocessed trauma and demons to fight suddenly thrust into being a father? It's a miracle he lasted as long as he did. What he needed was lovingkindness, extensive therapy, and knowing that though his

> **We all have stories. How we use our personal struggles and trials is everything.**

road wasn't easy and was filled with holes, God was right there to fill them up.

My sister and I visited him when I was seventeen and we maintained a close relationship on the phone for years. The best chapter of our story was when he was completely sober in my early twenties! But it didn't last. After four years of consistent sobriety (the longest he'd ever gone) and even becoming an Alcoholics Anonymous sponsor himself, he called me one day, intoxicated. And he lied about it when I questioned him. My son was only a few months old and, as I heard the slurring words on the phone with Anthony in my arms, I made the decision to end the call and any other attempts to build a relationship.

I was clear, if he was going to choose to drink I would not be around and he wouldn't be involved in my children's lives. They deserved better, and I was going to break the cycle of enabling that kind of relationship.

While we were not close, he did find the light of our Lord and went on to live a simple life on a farm. Though we didn't talk on the phone (something I maintained even though I forgave him, because he was still drinking after all), I would send him pictures of my babies, and he thoroughly enjoyed it all. In July of 2022, his ex-wife called to let me know he'd been diagnosed with an aggressive form of liver and lung cancer, which had spread throughout his body.

I knew what this meant. So, with my heart in my throat, I got on the phone with him for the first time in years. He sounded so tired and was clearly in pain. I told him I loved him and I'd be praying for healing. Just two months later, I'd be giving permission to remove his life support in order to allow him to pass through to heaven peacefully. The next day I'd fly to Idaho to take care of what little he had. A year prior, I promised I'd come see him again. Though it wasn't how I hoped, I kept my promise.

One day, when my children are older and can understand, I'll tell them the story.

And we all have stories.

How we use our personal struggles and trials is everything. Despite the memories I can't forget and the missing pieces of a family I couldn't have, I wouldn't change a thing. Every tear had its place and brought me right here. To you.

You'll find out quickly that I am slightly obsessed with Disney movies. I quote them often in my daily life. One of my favorites has origins from the movie *Dumbo*: "The very things that hold you down are going to lift you up, up, up!"[1]

In the military life, loneliness is going to grab ahold of you and try to weigh you down in its awfulness. But know this—if you do the work—you'll be using that dreaded memory for something really good. It's all about the journey, sweet friend.

Those who avoid addressing the underlying reasons for loneliness and box it up always find that box overflowing later. The mess it leaves after being hidden for so long is often worse than when it began, especially as it spills all over your life. Again, been there, done that, y'all!

I could go into a long-winded explanation of the importance of using healthy coping skills and not allowing destructive defense mechanisms to prevent emotional growth, but that would be another book in itself.

What I will tell you is that despite how hard it is to walk that path of raw processing and finding your healthy methods to cope, there is always beauty in the everlasting truth that you *can* work through it. "For I consider that the sufferings of this present time are not worth comparing with the glory that is to be revealed to us," Romans 8:18 tells us.

And you won't be alone when you do, I promise.

In order to tackle this beast of a feeling, you have to first understand what loneliness is, and what it's not.

THE CLINICAL AND SCIENTIFIC
HISTORY OF LONELINESS

In 1674, English naturalist John Ray compiled a glossary of infrequently used words. He included loneliness, which he defined as "far from neighbours."[2]

As a modern society, we have researched clinical implications of loneliness since the 1980s.[3] It was psychologist Frieda Fromm-Reichmann who first began considering loneliness as a mental health issue back in 1959. She described loneliness as overwhelmingly painful, disintegrative, and paralyzing.[4] Although she made questionable personal choices I'll skip over (no stone throwing and all that jazz), her work led to the explosion of the true clinical exploration into loneliness.

So, it's clear that we recognized the negative implications of being lonely because we were seeing it through evidence-based research and overall declining well-being as a society. Check. A published article in the *Indian Journal of Psychiatry* suggested it was an official disease, saying, "The pathological loneliness has its roots in medical model consisting of a host, an agent, and an environment and is thus, a disease."[5] The author's reasoning for this statement was in the way that loneliness affects our perception, thoughts, and even

> **God recognized the importance of avoiding loneliness, from the absolute beginning of time as we know it.**

the actual chemistry of our brains. Loneliness is a feeling and state of being that slowly eats away at us internally until it manifests physically. It is a powerful feeling. Remember what I said before about secrets making you sick? It's indisputable at this point.

We've examined the accepted definition and clinical implications of loneliness. But long before we had doctors and scientists researching the concept of loneliness, our Bible addressed it. Pretty eloquently, I might add!

Our ancestors were no strangers to loneliness, despite the formal official research only being recorded in more recent times. Though this section is truly devoted to clinical aspects, I just have to throw a little Bible epic-ness your way. Remember alllllllll the way back in Genesis when God was creating everything? Since God knows everything, it shouldn't surprise you that He recognized the importance of avoiding loneliness, from the absolute beginning of time as we know it!

No matter what version of the Bible you like to soak in, the realization that Adam wouldn't do well alone was glaringly obvious to God. We see evidence of its ramifications throughout the Bible later. Although I think (and hope) most of us aren't going through something quite as serious as some of those stories we find in those sacred pages, we all have our own battles with loneliness.

Don't compare or think your story is less than because someone else's sounds more challenging. *Your experience matters and needs space too.*

I also want to be absolutely clear on something as we continue to navigate the understanding of loneliness: there is a definitive difference between being by ourselves (solitude) and being *lonely*. The latter is a negative feeling, while the former is a healthy experience that can lead to improved self-confidence and worth. We should *absolutely* be okay sitting with ourselves and our thoughts from time to time. It gives us time to pause our hectic lives and be mindful of the beautiful moments we are living.

For example, I absolutely adore taking long hikes in the woods by myself (with supplies like bear mace; hey, I love the outdoors but I also appreciate the importance of staying alive). Breathing in God's beautiful creations and soaking up the peace of the forest resets me like nothing else. I *never* feel lonely in those moments, even though I am intentionally seeking solitude. But when my husband, Scott, was deployed and had to leave me in a strange city where I knew no one and had no support, I was so lonely it manifested into quite obvious physical symptoms of distress.

I couldn't eat without feeling sick, nothing in life gave me pleasure or joy, and I felt endlessly fatigued. *That* was loneliness morphing into a clinical episode of depression.

So, what exactly *is* this terrible feeling that so many of us are so deeply familiar with? Let's dissect it and lay it bare. According to the *Merriam-Webster Dictionary*, the word "lonely" refers to being cut off from others and having a "feeling of bleakness or desolation."[6] Psychologically, it refers to the absence of imperative social relations and a lack of affection or connections in current social relationships.[7] These explanations describe so many seasons of the military spouse's life that's it's eerie.

The official definitions or descriptions give us a good idea of what it feels like to experience loneliness, but we need to go a little deeper on how detrimental it can be for our well-being. I also want you to know and recognize the signs that it's rearing its head in your life and heart. Loneliness looks different for everyone, but there are definitely common themes or emotions that accompany this complex feeling. So, let's start with some of the specific types of loneliness we can experience as human beings. Though there is a plethora of opinions on the subject, these are the three that I feel bring the biggest negative impacts to our lives.[8]

Situational

Situational loneliness is exactly what it says and revolves around environmental factors. Examples include interpersonal conflicts, disasters, or migration (for us, this is a fancy word for moving, something we are deeply familiar with). Sadly, we'll probably all sit in this type of loneliness a time or two, or five. Situational can also equate to life stressors, something almost entirely unavoidable but more easily treatable.

Emotional

As human beings, we thrive on close emotional attachments. When that is missing, it can lead to loneliness, which can then spiral into a myriad of mental illness symptoms. This can accompany a loss of someone close to you who you had previously confided in and shared attachment with. Think about things like broken friendships, lost connections due to frequent moves, or any other force coming between you and a close attachment. It causes emotional weight like no other.

Social

Isolation and a lack of community support is detrimental. Emotional and social loneliness go hand in hand, each wreaking havoc on your health. This kind will arise when there is no sense of belonging or feeling valued. As creatures of God who were intended to thrive in families, groups, or communities, missing support and connection socially is perhaps the most harmful. In this type of loneliness, we will see isolation and declining health, and it is a road that takes a lot of work to find your way back home.

Experiencing any of these three forms of loneliness can bring about depression, feelings of worthlessness, anxiety, and physical symptoms such as reduced appetite and inability to sleep. While all this is occurring, our brains are shooting off stress hormones like cortisol, which is shortening our lifespan and making us physically ill.

Medical professionals openly discussed how many more patients they were seeing with headaches, muscle tension, or stomach problems, as the quarantines through the pandemic continued. We were not meant to be isolated as human beings and it was clearly witnessed as we watched the world shut down in 2020. Academic studies have even identified loneliness as a predictor of suicidal ideation and eventual attempts.[9]

When I say loneliness can be deadly, I mean it.

It's important to recognize the pattern of life-altering symptoms that can accompany extended loneliness and address the heart of what's going on before it progresses.

If you are experiencing loneliness, you are *not* alone. I pray working through it with me helps you in your path to processing and eventually healing.

Now that I've dragged you through some of my life, a brief history, and a clinical psychology lesson, I want to get to the really, really good stuff. This is your rainbow moment of the chapter (see, I *told* you it was coming). We are about to hit the part of our journey together that lights my heart on fire. Ready? Here we go.

THE BIBLICAL ANSWER TO LONELINESS

Ruth 1:1–5

Although there are many books of the Bible that make me nod my head, smile, and feel joy, Ruth is special. You know how you can watch a movie ten times and find something new each time? The Bible is like that for me. I'd heard and read the story of Ruth many times growing up, but it wouldn't be until I had been a military spouse for over fifteen years that I saw the parallels of our lives. I firmly believe that God revealed it to me only when I was ready.

When you dive into the book of Ruth, remember that it takes place during a time period when the judges ruled the people of Israel. At this time, the nation did not have a king, so the judges' duties were basically to govern under God's direction: drive out their enemies, lead the people in God's law, and so on.

We see Naomi's husband, Elimelech, move her and their two

sons, Mahlon and Chilion, from Judah to Moab because of the on-going famine. To give a little context, Moabites were pagans. So, here's Naomi in a strange land with only her sons and husband as her community when they arrive. Add in the factor of no true connection spiritually, and it was certainly a small circle of support. Lonely.

Eventually her husband dies.

But she still has her two sons, and although I imagine she was sad she pressed on. Both sons had married Moabite women, Orpah, and our honorary military soul sister, Ruth. They were all a unit until Mahlon and Chilion died.

Suddenly, Naomi was thrust into the pit of loss and pain all over again. This time she felt (I think) like there was no hope or goodness left, lost without the physical presence of her family. This belief is supported by the undertones of bitterness we feel in her words and anger with God we see later on in the story. Here, we recognize what Naomi is going through: loneliness.

She was probably experiencing all three types of loneliness that we covered earlier. *Situational* (migration to Moab away from support), *emotional* (loss of family), and *social* (isolation and lack of community). Naomi was going through it, y'all, but what she doesn't realize yet is that she won't have to do it on her own.

God used a pagan woman with no blood ties to Naomi in order to restore her faith in Him, love her, and show the true meaning of lovingkindness.

This is it, friends.

You *will* go through seasons of loneliness that challenge everything you believe to be good. Some of these trials will make you question where God is leading you and even make you doubt His love or—maybe even worse—His existence. There is no judging here. We have all been there in some form or another. And if you meet a Christian who hasn't even had a moment or sliver of a shadow of doubt, I *need* to meet them. Over a cup of coffee, of course.

But guess what? Despite your internal ache of loneliness, you are *never* alone. God is always with you, ready to bring you through your despair.

First Peter 5:10 is encouraging: "And after you have suffered a little while, the God of all grace, who has called you to his eternal glory in Christ, will himself restore, confirm, strengthen, and establish you."

God is with you, friend.

I often use music as a positive tool to combat bad moods and struggles I'm going through. But just know that although I love Jesus with my whole heart, I rock out hard to some '90s hip-hop too. It's typically country music I like, but I grew up alongside Tupac and it is what it is. But at this moment, I am *actually* listening to one of my favorite worship songs, and its words are so poignant for this. I encourage you to listen to and look up the lyrics to the beautiful song "Oh My Soul" as sung by Casting Crowns.[10]

To me, this song is telling us to keep on keeping on. Yes, what you are sitting with is hard. *It hurts.* But just like the sun rises, it will set too. Work through it one moment at a time and know what's waiting for you when you come out of it.

He sits with us as our shoulders shake with those sobs that echo our pain. I like to imagine that when we've exhausted our tears, it's His hand on our head that gives the relief that often accompanies emotional unburdening. He was certainly sitting with Ruth in hers, giving her the strength she needed to overcome loneliness not only for herself but for Naomi too.

Lovingkindness is a *hope* we desperately need! Paired with God's perfect and constantly present love, you *will* heal your loneliness. And as we continue to navigate the story of Ruth together, I'll show you how.

Let's Talk about It

Matthew 28:20 tells us, "Behold, I am with you always, to the end of the age."

As we delve into the topic of loneliness, it is my fervent hope you begin to hold fast to the realization that He is with us, in and through everything. As a clinician I believe deeply in the power of sharing stories and the healing that can result from the unburdening. So right now, write down the thing in your life that is making you feel the deepest loneliness and heartache. Then, head over to Romans 5:1–5. There I pray you find some restoration of peace . . . and a whole lot of love.

2

FINDING CONNECTIONS

Since military spouses move an average of every two to three years, connecting and building our circle is usually done at warp speed. As a matter of fact, it's laughingly known for most of us as "friend-speed-dating." If you have an immediate wild vision in your brain of loudly buzzing timers and humans moving around through a musical chairs sort of environment, then yes. That's it!

It may sound intense or highly dramatic, but it's something mutually agreed upon and accepted, making finding friends much easier. Once the majority of us have unpacked and organized our home and family and found a hairdresser (very important), seeking our circle of people is usually next on the list. It's almost innate within us to find connection. With the lives we lead, support and community are necessary for stress mitigation and combating—you guessed it—loneliness.

Our civilian brothers and sisters can typically trace their friendship circle back decades by the time they are well into their forties. Maybe their childhood friends are still on speed dial (my inner '90s child is showing here). But our circle could be just a few weeks old and you'd never guess. It's one of our secret powers as military spouses.

I firmly think this is because of our shared history before we even meet. As human beings, we engage in homophily, which is the tendency for people to seek out or be attracted to those who are similar to themselves.[1]

Remember the saying "birds of a feather flock together"? Simply put, we seek out what we know and feel comfortable with. This includes values or beliefs. Church is a perfect example. As a Christian I wouldn't go to a sanctuary where the belief and hope in Jesus wasn't absolute. The same can be said for how military spouses roll. If we have children, we tend to seek out friends who have children. Likewise, when we enjoy certain social events, it's often because others who attend are probably relatable to us.

And we never know how beautiful it is to have it until we don't.

Truthfully, the hardest move we ever made was to an area without other military spouses. We lived seventy miles and over an hour from the Coast Guard cutter (vessel) he was on and the nearest military base. Though this living arrangement made sense at the time because we were saving money for our future, it was *so* hard.

These were terrible, no good, very bad days.

I spent a lot of time renting Blockbuster movies (okay—*Grey's Anatomy*, seasons one through three repeatedly, if I'm being truly transparent) and crying on the couch. In holey and questionably dirty clothing, I might add. Eventually I made friends when I started working, but for a while life wasn't very pleasant.

> **The deep need to forge connections is nothing new for any of us because, remember, God knew from the beginning we couldn't be alone.**

The weight of loneliness followed me everywhere I went. Picture a cartoon character with a perpetual raincloud over its head. That was me because I was deeply missing the connection to my husband and my family. Occasional phone calls weren't enough, and it was obvious.

The deep need to forge connections is nothing new for any of us because, remember, God *knew* from the beginning we couldn't be alone. Really, He didn't want anyone to be alone! Even animals were created in pairs. When you factor in all the elements causing loneliness, it makes sense that the more connected we feel, the less lonely we are too. Let's get into the epic science and neuropathy of social connections.

THE CLINICAL ANSWER AND
SCIENCE OF CONNECTION

According to a meta-analysis by Julianne Holt-Lunstad and colleagues at Brigham Young University, low social interaction was likened to smoking fifteen cigarettes a day and being more harmful than not exercising.[2] Holy smokes. Pun intended.

A host of other public studies demonstrate the shocking impact of lack of connection. Higher blood pressure, obesity, and shorter lifespan are prevalent outcomes in those without a circle of support. Researchers have also found higher rates of isolation, depression, and anxiety.

This revelation isn't anything new, though. In Maslow's hierarchy of needs, we see social connection referenced and its importance labeled "love and belongingness."[3] Though I don't aspire to completely follow any one theory, the triangle he presents makes sense in my mind and I hope in yours too. Countless researchers, scientists, and psychiatrists have pored over and through this concept. They've all discovered the same thing: we need each other.

It starts in infancy.

A newborn baby's only goal after birth is quite literally to survive. Without means of communicating, she cries—loudly and often, I might add. The sound should trigger a release of oxytocin in her mother's brain, which is also known as the bonding hormone. It signals a let-down reflex in nursing mamas as well as an immediate need to soothe the baby. When a baby isn't cared for well or doesn't feel connected and secure, it leads to what is commonly known as "failure to thrive."

This concept or label isn't only found in neglected or isolated babies, either.

The same bonding hormone we see in mothers has been found to be released when we hug others, hold hands, or engage in certain marital, ahem, bedroom activities.

The bonding hormone we feel when we are connecting to our loved ones does a whole bunch of pretty epic things. It combats the nasty hormones we experience during anxiety or depression (with my husband gone and no one around, my pitiful state makes sense), pairs up with serotonin (think mood regulation) and dopamine, which is known as the pleasure hormone.

This isn't just found within the private marital bedroom fun either—personally, my brain lights up with it for chocolate; I admit it without shame. Sort of.

Oxytocin is pretty amazing, isn't it? And it all begins when we feel a sense of belonging as we connect with others. To bring it all home, we've been hardwired as human beings to connect to others, and it's been proven through endless research (and God's infinite wisdom, of course) that without connection, life isn't very fun. And in fact, we all suffer.

Physically, emotionally—and spiritually.

THE BIBLICAL ANSWERS FOR
CONNECTION TO FIGHT LONELINESS

Ruth 1:6–18

When we last left the story of Ruth, Naomi was in despair over the loss of not only her husband but now her only two sons. No longer feeling like she belonged, especially in the foreign land, she had to make some tough decisions. Their deaths would be the catalyst that would lead her to recognize she needed to return to Judah. There was nothing left for her in Moab. Though she initially set out with her daughters-in-law beside her, she eventually stopped them. "Go, return each of you to her mother's house," she told them (Ruth 1:8).

And this right here is where I was shocked reading it as an adult.

> In the midst of refusing to leave Naomi, Ruth said the words that military spouses know and should recognize deep within their souls: "Where you go I will go."

In these pages of Ruth we find a woman truly alone in the world. The only two people Naomi had left she tried to send away so she could go on a road trip back home and go alone. I choose to see this as a good deed. She was saving Orpah and Ruth from her own fate of leaving everything she had known behind. She released them from their obligation and back into their own supports and community.

But her action can also be viewed as a clinical response to loneliness. Naomi, whose family consisted of these two women related to her only by marriage, was isolating herself even further. Sound familiar? We tend to do this to people when we aren't feeling so hot about ourselves or our lives either. We push everyone away.

Though I am adding to the story a bit, I really feel like Naomi knew what life would be like for them. Bound to a family without sons, the opportunity for children or a real future was bleak. We see *lovingkindness* right here in the midst of Naomi's bitterness and disconnect. Even as she raged against God and her current life, she prayed for Orpah and Ruth. "May the LORD deal kindly with you," she said. "The LORD grant that you may find rest" (Ruth 1:8–9).

Orpah would return to Moab in tears after putting up a small amount of resistance, but Ruth could not be deterred from staying with her mother-in-law, regardless of how Naomi pleaded for her to go. In the midst of refusing Naomi, she said the words that military spouses know and should recognize deep within their souls: "Where you go I will go" (Ruth 1:16).

Seeing this kind of devotion and love in what is essentially a friendship between the two women is beautiful. It's something we live by with our spouses while we spend years following them endlessly around the globe as they serve. It's a loving connection that has the power to withstand so much adversity and heartache, because we do it together.

If you need any further proof of the strength of God's pulling you toward Him and His strength for your needs, Ruth brings you right to the heart of it. With her steadfast and immediate love for our God, despite her pagan upbringing, all through her connection to Naomi—how can we not feel it? Powerful and indisputable truth, hope, and love. All wrapped in His Word.

If human connections have been proven to scientifically begin with happy hormones and like-mindedness, we should always be able to find that sense of belonging in God. Without fail, He will carry us through, because the loving connection we share with Him is always present. Though there are many beautiful stories that show evidence of this phenomenon throughout our Bible, we see the majestic power of God's promise of "belonging" or "connection" unfold on those long crossroads between Moab and Judah.

Through Ruth—and God, of course—Naomi was pulled from her bitter and broken pit of loneliness to the realization that she was never alone. And neither are you, sweet friend.

Because where you go . . . so does your beautiful and unbreakable connection to God.

Let's Talk about It

You've been doing some work and let me tell you, building connections *is* work. But I promise it'll all be worth it in the end! Romans 8:28 says, "And we know that for those who love God all things work together for good, for those who are called according to his purpose." I fervently believe each connection we make in our lives, whether for a season or forever, was ordained by Him and intentionally purposeful. What is the hardest part of forging new connections for you? Write it down in your journal, my friend. After you do, spend some time in James 1:2–6. Sometimes I think we profess our faith in Him and His plan, but still harbor seeds of doubt in the exact unfolding of the plan. James reminds us that one who continually doubts is "like a wave of the sea that is driven and tossed by the wind." Be a strong ship in those seas, filled with unsinkable faith.

3

GUARDING YOUR HEART

I don't want you to be misled by the title of this chapter. This doesn't mean to close yourself off or isolate yourself, because it would absolutely defeat working through loneliness. Instead, I want you to think of those words as a way to prepare for loss and the eventual feeling of disconnection or unbelonging (loneliness) we'll all face in life. They are all part of what clinicians like to term as life stressors, and there is no escaping them.

But you can be armed and ready.

When I think of the word *prep*, my military spouse brain immediately goes to creating a "go bag." If your mind is wandering into daydreams of doomsday preppers—yes! Perfect analogy.

Seriously. But I don't want you digging an underground bunker (unless you really want to). Instead, I want you to do it metaphorically, in your mind.

But before you grab a shovel for our imagined bunker, let's dig into a little bit of the clinical aspects of what guarding your heart should look like.

When we moved from Florida to Alaska, it was hard. Long-distance calls were expensive (I'm *that* old) and I was feeling a little lost. But by this point, I had been at this military life for a few years and dug in quickly. Within months, I made a friend who called to my soul and who I couldn't live without!

We finished each other's sentences, had more fun than I can put into words, and connected in a way I never prepared for. My husband's orders were for three years, so we had plenty of time to create memories, right?

Wrong. The admiral he was working for was transferring to Virginia—and asked Scott to go. It was an honor and would get us back to the East Coast and closer to family. He said yes and just fourteen months after we arrived in Alaska, we left.

I never guarded my heart for this because I thought I had time to get ready. But that's the military for you (and life). Anything can happen. Our airport goodbye was loud, filled with tears, and absolutely heartbreaking. It took months for me to work through my sadness and loneliness without her.

It was a lesson I took with me to every duty station thereafter. Now, don't get me wrong. I am still my loud, extroverted self, seeking friends everywhere we go. But internally I use tools to remind myself that where I am is temporary. This means I'm careful about getting deeply attached to our homes, friends, or surroundings, because I know my roots will have to be uprooted and replanted.

Don't allow the temporary nature of our lives let you miss out on the good, though. It will hurt when you say goodbye. I won't sugarcoat it. But the chapter of your story with these friends and places and experiences in it? So worth it.

> **The word grit means courage, resolve, and strength of character, and it transformed how I looked at internally creating readiness and fortitude for life.**

The word *resiliency* sounds like a positive, right? But it's been tragically overused within our military community. For many, it tends to bring on visible cringing or even epic eye rolls. We don't mean to be rude, but hearing how resilient we are all the time when internally we tend to resemble a slowly erupting volcano touches a nerve or two. So, let's scratch resiliency.

Instead, I am going to borrow another word that more adequately describes how we should approach life: with unwavering and unapologetic *grit*. I'll publicly thank my sweet Army chaplain spouse and licensed counselor friend, Corie Weathers, for it. *Grit* transformed how I looked at internally creating readiness and fortitude for life. The word itself means courage, resolve, and strength of character.

But you can have all of these things and still fall apart from time to time.

As military spouses we are built to be *scrappy*. This word more clearly identifies what we hope to aspire to than resiliency ever could. *This* is the kind of doomsday prepping I want to process with you! The scrappy kind, friends.

But instead of getting ready for the end of the world, we'll prep for tackling icky feelings and ongoing unavoidable life stressors—guarding our hearts as we go along.

THE CLINICAL UNDERSTANDING OF GUARDING YOUR HEART OR BUILDING GRIT

As a therapist, I often tell my younger clients, as we work through their trauma, how much I wish I could wave a magic wand and protect them from future hurt forever. I hurt when they hurt. But I can't create that wand for anyone.

Of course, I pray for it anyway because so many of them are so little with such big and ugly experiences no one deserves to navigate and process as a child. After I say my piece about "no magic," I add that I am absolutely building them a toolbox to not only work through their current hardship but to have for the future stressors—guarding their hearts and readying them for the battles I know will come.

Because, sweet friend, life will bring us these hardships without fail.

I want you to take this chapter to start building what I call the proverbial guard-your-heart toolbox. It'll help you work through any current loneliness and negative feelings you are experiencing but will also be readying you for the future experiences.

Now, where should all of this prep work begin? Truthfully—in our childhood.

As children, we begin learning positive coping mechanisms pretty early on. For instance, when a baby or toddler becomes upset, he seeks comfort from his parents or guardians. Young children or adolescents will learn to engage in activities that bring joy. They don't even realize how in those actions, grit is developing right along with their go-to guard-your-heart toolbox.

If a child is lucky enough to have both healthy role models (look up social learning theory, which explains a lot of what I am trying to convey here) and positive environment, their ability to not only work through existing stressors is secured, but the toolbox for the future events looks pretty stinking bright too.

However, it's definitely not always the case. In fact, the adverse childhood experience (ACE) is prevalent in society. The Centers for Disease Control (CDC) says that ACEs are potentially traumatic events that occur in childhood (0–17 years) and estimates around 61 percent of adults have experienced one ACE in their lifetime. And one in six have experienced four or more.[1]

These numbers should make you ache.

The list of ACEs includes divorce, death, all sorts of ugly abuse, witnessing substance use and addiction, and more. Without initial and immediate support to work through these, outcomes are statistically heartbreaking. Multiple studies and the CDC themselves have proven children who grow within traumatic environments have difficulty forming stable and healthy relationships.

Full disclosure, I have ACEs of my own: abuse, household challenges, divorce, incarcerated parent, mental illness, and substance use. Other ACEs in addition to those on the CDC's list include poverty, racism, different kinds of violence. On a growing brain and child, these experiences leave lasting impact.

It's toxic stress.

I delve into all of this to paint a picture of the world and how adults we know and love are already walking through it. Now add the stress of being in an active-duty military marriage and life.

See where I am going with this?

Now, we know more than half the world already has a traumatic history. Let's dive into the military. The US Army Recruiting Command asked RAND Arroyo to conduct a survey on enlisted personnel to examine the why behind joining. It should be no surprise that 17 percent of those surveyed enlisted to escape a negative home environment.[2]

A better life, or escape, is something you'll hear frequently within the enlisted forces, regardless of branch of service. From 2016 through 2019, my husband was stationed in Cape May, New Jersey—home to the United States Coast Guard Training Center.

In other words, coastie boot camp.

I wish I could tell you these young babies (okay, they weren't babies but for us thirty- and forty-somethings, they sure felt like our children) showed up bright-eyed and fully supported by family and friends. In fact, so many came to us to get *away* from their life. We even had quite a few who were homeless as they entered the gates.

Living in their cars or couch-to-couch is a part of the federal definition of homelessness. Then after eight or twelve weeks (depending on branch of service) they are thrust into the big world to defend Americans from foreign and domestic threats.

As a clinician I can tell you without a doubt, those who've never unpacked their lives or built toolboxes struggle and they don't often do it very well. They also tend to get married young.

I am setting the stage to understanding it all, trust me. We're almost there!

Continually moving around for the military mission, greatly reducing the ability to build a support network? Check. Potential for introducing trauma due to position within the armed forces? Check. Statistical chances of already carrying trauma without a toolbox? Check. Add in the likelihood of maladaptive coping mechanisms like alcohol, which is readily consumed in the military culture? Check.

> **Regardless of where you are in your life's journey, you need to have a toolbox to guard your heart for this big world and life.**

It's a reality I can't minimize, friend.

We're built as humans for connection, belonging, and community. It was also intended for us to grow up nurtured and loved. Maybe you did and I love it for you.

Or maybe you were like me and so many others who didn't.

Regardless of where you are in your life's journey, you *need* to have a toolbox to guard your heart for this big world and life.

Fill it with things like physical activity, music, laughter, and talk therapy (this can be with a professional or within peer-to-peer networks, but just talk). There is no cookie-cutter approach to this. If it brings you joy while helping you process those life stressors we can't avoid, throw it in your guard-your-heart box. Now the best part. Ready?

God is holding the biggest tool for connection we so desperately need!

THE BIBLICAL ANSWER TO
GUARDING YOUR HEART OR BUILDING GRIT

Ruth 1:19–21

When we last left the book of Ruth, her grit was witnessed in all its blinding glory. Despite her mother-in-law and elder telling her to do something (these things were a big deal back then), she didn't.

Instead, she outright refused.

She pulled that strength of character like a shield and did what was on her heart. Her refusal was so passionate that Naomi didn't ask again.

Grit.

Here's where it starts to get really interesting. The women finally reached Bethlehem and we see the townspeople reacting. In today's modern world I would paint a picture of matrons sitting around spilling the tea, maybe outright gossiping about Naomi and Ruth—hopefully not too unkindly.

Remember, Naomi left during hard times—a famine. Already a no-no, but she also fled to an outright pagan land. Epic no-no. Now she returns alone with a Moabite daughter-in-law who's presumably a pagan?

So. Much. Tea.

Anyway, we really see Naomi's anger in those moments. One woman asked, "Hey, is that really Naomi?" and her reply was a stinger.

"Do not call me Naomi [the name Naomi means pleasant]; call me Mara, for the Almighty has dealt very bitterly with me. I went away full, and the LORD has brought me back empty. Why call me Naomi, when the LORD has testified against me and the Almighty has brought calamity upon me?" (Ruth 1:20–21).

Let's unpack this. The word *mara* is of Hebrew origin and means bitter.[3] Whoa, she really went there. But it gets worse; calamity in Hebrew is pretty serious, connoting disaster, tragedy, catastrophe, suffering, and such.

So, to sum it up—we see Naomi blaming God for every wrong she experienced after leaving. Did you know the reason the family fled to Moab in the first place, the famine, was sometimes seen as a chastisement from God and a demonstration of His great disappointment in His people's choices? One could assume how running away from God's consequences could cause even further hardship . . . not unlike a stubborn child refusing to accept responsibility and prolonging being grounded.

I'm definitely talking about my own two children. My prayers for patience usually revolve around them.

Kidding. Sort of.

Anyway, back to the good stuff.

Here's where I want to connect it all for you, friend. We cannot escape or run away from the things in our life bringing us sadness, challenges, or other uncomfortable circumstances. This is a defense mechanism hardwired within all of us as part of our humanness. You know it as "sweeping it all under the rug" or "tabling it for another day." Clinically, it's known as suppression or avoidance. The problem with running away from messy things? It all comes back like a boomerang. And with a bang, I might add.

Though the losses Naomi experienced due to her lack of faith or obedience in God are heartbreaking to read through, there is beauty in it. Why? Because our Almighty didn't give up on her, even in the face of some pretty strong language. Instead of turning His back, He gave her a companion to not only sit with her in the dark pit of loneliness and heartache but pull her out to the other side. And—back to Him.

God did a whole lot more, but I won't skip ahead. Friends, there's such incredibly good news coming (there's definitely a hint in there—I am terrible with surprises) and all through the bad, ugly, and hard the promise is there.

When I talk about guarding our hearts with the toolbox and building grit, stories like Ruth's are absolutely part of it being successful. But even more, there's a deep lesson in this. I showed you all the clinical information and walked with you through Ruth, but now you get the grand finale.

The best part of our toolbox to prepare for life's hardships and build grit? Our awesome, amazing, and patient God. Let Him be your strength when you think you have none—there's nothing too big for Him. His Word should always be the way we build the foundation of that imagined shield for guarding our hearts or developing our grit to tackle life. The rest of the things we do to prepare and cope are the figurative nuts and bolts of support. He is the deep and strong foundation we build it all upon.

God is our true secret weapon to tackling all the hard stuff—and winning.

Let's Talk about It

Guarding your heart against hurt takes time and a whole lot of internal processing. But guess what? You can do this with your Bible in hand, which is sure to help guide you through your journey. I shared some of my hardest moments in childhood and how they impacted me for years after. I wonder if you, too, are holding on to some hurts inside your heart as you navigate this book. Though it may be one of the hardest things you've done, I'd like you to write those down. Why? Because it's imperative we acknowledge the things weighing us down, no matter how long ago they occurred in our lives. This may not come without tears or heaviness in your heart. But Jesus has some comfort for you! Read Matthew 11:27–30 and be comforted in knowing He can hold our hurt. And be the way to heal it.

4

WADING THROUGH MILITARY LIFE

At this point in our journey together, you're getting to know me. I drink too much coffee and watch a lot of Disney movies. But another fun fact about me: I love using water terminology for navigating life, and this chapter title is no exception.

I'm embarrassed to admit this but here it is. I didn't *know* what the Coast Guard was on my first date in 2005 with Scott. To dig myself even deeper in embarrassment, I was raised in Florida—home to one of the biggest areas of responsibility for the service.

Oops.

I made up for it by doing things like willingly taking courses on maritime history and becoming their biggest cheerleader! I even fought with a professor (and won) regarding the absolute and indisputable fact that the Coast Guard is a branch of the military. Hence using water terminology, probably. Always ready (if you know, you know).

Wading means to walk with effort. If the ocean current pulls you out, fiercely fighting the waves will tire you quickly. But wading... well, that's what we are taught to do to stay alive in this situation. One meaning of the Old English word *wadan* is to "move onward."[1]

With the crazy waves and undertow, the military life will absolutely bring this as a vital skill, which will support your journey in a healthy way. It's the fortitude you need to just keep swimming (*Finding Nemo* quotes are the best, y'all) and not tire out or give in.

Using this tool came early for me because of my clinical background, but one I still grab on to like an oar every single time we PCS (permanent change of station) or move. The stress of starting over creeps up over you, like a wave. I learned this lesson the hard way during the first few moves.

I'd find myself bickering with my husband for no reason at all. He could look at me wrong and I'd melt down like he committed an unforgivable transgression. It was bananas! Finally I figured out I was bottling everything up inside and eventually exploding like a shaken-up soda pop.

First, realizing the things you won't be around for as your time to move grows near. Then the endless lists you begin to make so nothing of importance gets forgotten in the hustle and bustle of the process. Eventually, you see all the things around you and can find yourself drowning if you aren't careful.

My own personal stressors usually revolved around my fears of being able to find employment (I had always felt deeply about contributing to our family and household) and of course to our kiddos and their needs. The anxiety I would experience was crippling!

These days my husband and I communicate all our feelings and worries. As I type these words, we're going through it now. Over a good backyard fire, I let it all out. It's a battle we've learned to fight together, and communication is at the heart of it.

Letting it out doesn't completely erase the mental worry list, but it eases my burden and makes it easier to work through and work toward. Because among these things are all of the feelings and emotions this season will bring. Do me a favor? Talk about it.

CLINICAL UNDERSTANDING OF
WADING THROUGH MILITARY LIFE

Clinically, what I mean by wading is to process or unpack all your "stuff." We've worked through what loneliness is, the importance of connections, and guarding your heart with that handy toolbox. With all of those important pieces of the puzzle, the skill of wading can come in. How can you be ready for the next thing or combat your current icky feelings if you never dig into their why or talk about them? Let's get right to airing alllllllll the dirty laundry, friend.

"Let it go, let it go, can't hold it back anymore!"[2] (I realllllllly love Disney movies).

Back to wading. Healing through wading is more than just talking about your issues, but intentionally taking an event or challenge that has brought on negative feelings and dissecting it. Piece by piece. You know how a mechanic will take an engine apart to find the source of the problem? Or how a surgeon has to cut through the skin and muscle to reach the area they need to operate on? Those are pictures of us as human beings processing.

When I was feeling depressed during the height of my loneliness as a military spouse, simply saying I felt empty and sharing that I wasn't finding joy wasn't enough. Saying these things out loud is simply expressing or verbalizing feelings. Instead, I examined those feelings and the triggering events and then worked to understand why I was so miserable. Once I did the work, it didn't take long to figure out the root of it all.

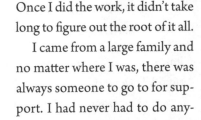

When you are sitting in the dark pit of loneliness, stagnancy is even more uncomfortable and damaging than trying something new.

I came from a large family and no matter where I was, there was always someone to go to for support. I had never had to do anything alone and had never lived outside of my hometown. Suddenly being thrust into a new city and left by myself was the trigger for all of those feelings. I was a fish out of water (see what I did there?).

It took me some time to recognize I had essentially become codependent on having company and ever-present support. Adjusting to everything being the opposite was a shock for me, leading to those negative feelings. Once I understood why I was feeling that way and when I processed it all, I was ready to do work.

Processing isn't always easy or pretty either. Bringing up things you'd previously buried means you are re-exposing yourself to them, which can hurt. A lot. But without unpacking everything to understand it, nothing changes. When you are sitting in the dark pit of loneliness, stagnancy is even more uncomfortable and damaging than trying something new.

Although I highly encourage you to seek out a therapist to walk with you through this, it isn't a must for wading successfully. You'll find a ton of free resources on the internet to assist you with recognizing patterns and maladaptive coping mechanisms and understanding where your triggers are. Psychologytoday .com and Therapistaid.com are both filled with great resources.

Consider journaling about what you are pulling out from under your rug. It doesn't mean you have to go crazy writing, for those of you who don't necessarily enjoy it. The goal is just to empty out the things on your mind and heart, making them visible and tangible to target.

When you have a negative thought about yourself or the event/issue you are processing, replace it with something positive.

Journaling will help you express your thoughts in a clearer way, and it's another tool to go back to later on. From there, this will give you the space to tackle negative assumptions and give yourself grace for each experience or feeling. I am a huge fan of thought reframing, which is a technique used in cognitive behavioral therapy.

When you have a negative thought about yourself or the event/issue you are processing, replace it with something positive.

For a long time, I would think about the terrible mistakes I made as I grew into myself. I replayed them like a bad record inside my head. The guilt or shame would eat away at me, bringing my mood even further down in the dumps. What I learned to do was reframe those thoughts as they came in. I'd think things like, *You did this because of x, y, z. You've grown and will use the lesson in this hardship to do better.*

It took a lot of work and, truthfully, it was similar to exposure therapy in that the more I practiced it, the more the ache inside eased as I had those thoughts. Thought reframing can be arduous work, but eventually we teach our brains (and our whole selves) to be healthier. Isn't it crazy how we can so easily find empathy and give grace to others rather than ourselves?

Here's where I want you to remember the oxygen mask analogy. You can't help others if you can't catch *your* breath, right? As any good Italian will tell you, *first* comes the pasta and *then* the salad.

So, my friend, make sure you breathe. And do it well.

THE BIBLICAL ANSWER TO
WADING THROUGH MILITARY LIFE

Ruth 2:1–7

I just love getting to this part. So many of the answers we seek can be found in God's Word. Isn't the feeling just amazing when a passage you've read hundreds of times suddenly causes a light bulb of understanding to go off or answers a question you've longed for the answer to? The story of Ruth has done this for me so many times.

As you navigate this chapter, I pray the message within its pages brings light for you.

Although we have good dialog in this account we find in the book of Ruth, there's nothing about Naomi or Ruth journaling their feelings or talking through them. But where I will pull an analogy for you is in how they moved onward after settling in Bethlehem. You didn't see these women cower inside or avoid living, right? Ruth quickly got to work and went to the fields.

Now, I know it was work or starve in those days, but the choice for how to respond to circumstances was there. They chose to wade and get the work done. Here's another *aha* moment for you: Isn't it ironic that Naomi left during a famine and as she returns, it's during what appears to be a rich harvest? Something to think about—He has His ways.

All right, so Ruth is all in on going to work to provide for her and Naomi. I won't shy away from all the kind of work she was hoping to do: getting noticed. We learn she was trying to find favor in the eyes of the owner of those barley fields, who was a distant family relation of Naomi's; the man was a "kinsman redeemer."

Now Naomi had a relative of her husband's, a worthy man of the clan of Elimelech, whose name was Boaz. And Ruth the Moabite said to Naomi, "Let me go to the field and glean among the ears of grain after him in whose sight I shall find favor." And she said to her, "Go, my daughter." So she set out and went and gleaned in the field after the reapers, and she happened to come to the part of the field belonging to Boaz, who was of the clan of Elimelech. (Ruth 2:1–3)

Back then, a widow would be destitute without a man supporting her. There weren't employment opportunities or options for self-efficiency, and it was up to the family of her deceased husband to provide for her.

"Slow is fast and fast is slow"—a great military saying I love to borrow. Another is to find a way to "work the problem."

We meet Boaz in this part of the story, but what I really want you to take note of is how Ruth approached this season of her life. She was clear in what she had to do, but she didn't show up in a red dress and fiercely declare her intentions, right? No, she was wading through instead. "Slow is fast and fast is slow"—a great military saying I love to borrow.

Another is to find a way to "work the problem." It's a familiar saying from one of my favorite shows, *SEAL Team*. If you look closely, "work the problem" is so relatable to the challenges we face as military spouses. The lesson in this section of your challenge is the way you approach it.

Attitude can be everything.

Sure, there are times we have something added to our plates that makes us want to smash it. Hard. But in the end, all you'll have is anger and broken pieces to clean up. But when we take deep breaths (breathing well is indisputably linked to reduced depression and anxiety symptoms, by the way), change our thoughts, and channel our energy into the good, our challenging chapter or season has the power to write a completely different ending than what we envisioned.

Now Boaz was described in this section as "a worthy man." This is a big word in the Bible. In Hebrew, the word is *zakah* and when you are doing it for God, it means to make oneself pure, to keep pure or to make oneself clean and morally pure as a characteristic.[3] This guy had it going on, y'all.

Ruth then gets permission and heads to the fields in hopes that in his sight she would find favor. She took time to put all of the puzzle pieces in place so that Boaz saw her for who she really was (wading was happening for sure).

Ruth was such a faithful woman, filled to the brim with lovingkindness through everything she did and faced. Remember, she was still a Moabite, she was a widow, and she would have been thought of as less than because of her pagan roots. But don't forget—we bloom wherever we are planted, and our roots have the power to shift and continue on, even when they are cut off at the knees.

Despite having all of this assumed baggage, which in those days definitely didn't win immediate favor in the eyes of many, she believed she could save not only Naomi but herself. And she did it. She had some serious grit and a whole lot of goodness. And slowly wading, she moved onward.

And you will too.

Let's Talk about It

I want you to reflect on that oxygen mask analogy as we reflect on wading through life. As human beings, we're typically so quick to help others but don't often take the time to offer the same grace to ourselves and the things we're going through. Social media can absolutely reinforce unrealistic expectations of life, with a good portion of people sharing only beautiful pictures. Here I'd like you to reflect on something going on in your life that *you* need help with. After you do that, I want you to jot down three things in your journal that bring you joy. Pick one of them and commit to doing it, at least two times a week. I won't go into the pouring from an empty cup analogy because you've heard it time and time again. Instead, I'm going to tell you something simple. Choose joy.

5

GOD'S LOVE

Okay then, we've been busy working through loneliness in these first few chapters! We've navigated how loneliness impacts your life in negative ways, but in and through all of it, those feelings should be pushing us closer to God's love.

It's the one constant we can count on regardless of the chaos swirling around us. As a Florida girl, I absolutely appreciate the cheesy ability to refer to life as a hurricane and place our God as the calm or eye in the storm. Here's what I learned about the eye of the storm: "Skies are often clear above the eye and winds are relatively light. It is actually the calmest section of any hurricane. The eye is so calm because the now strong surface winds that converge toward the center never reach it."[1]

As long as you remain within it, you're okay. And guess what? Remember this:

His love is the eye of our storm, always.

There are times it's easy to forget this. I admit that freely. There have been moments of undeniable grief in my life that have caused me to question Him. Why would He allow these terrible things to happen to me? How could He look on as I lost the things I loved most? Where was His unwavering love in all of it?

> **His love is the eye of our storm, always.**

My first experience with questioning came when I was thirteen years old. Remember that uncle I told you about—who raised me as his own? He went to work one day and, without warning, had a massive heart attack. He died instantly on the floor, despite all everyone around him tried to do to revive him.

For a young girl who'd already been through undeniable trauma and loss, I couldn't process it. My grief was crippling. I remember running from the house and walking for hours, just crying and raging at God for taking him from me.

It would take months for me to find my way back to God and His Word. My grandmother remained a constant, reminding me that we'll never truly understand why things happen the way they do. But in the end, the hard and bad things will disappear, and we'll be with God in heaven for eternity if we've chosen to follow Jesus as our Savior.

My grandmother was patient too. She never pushed me or shamed me for my feelings against my faith. Why? She, too, had walked that path during hardship. So, she believed for me and ensured I felt His love—even when I was blind to it. I'd need that lesson to pull from my toolbox later, when I lost my grandfather the day after I turned seventeen. But by the time I lost my grandmother in 2019, I could see His hands holding me and showing me the light in the darkness. Her last words in the hospital were profound:

"I'm going home!"

Of course I wanted more time with her. Despite her diagnosis of terminal cancer and her rapidly advancing dementia, I wanted every moment possible to hold her hand, look into her beautiful hazel eyes, and feel her breathe.

Even in the midst of my broken heart, I could see God's gift to me. It was His voice inside that pushed me to go home to her in the first place. It created a ripple of events that hurts my heart even today to remember—but there was beauty in it too.

Hooked up to endless wires in the hospital, she was so pale against the sterile sheets, I asked her if she knew who I was. It had been a year since she could remember. I'll never forget her crooked smile and shining eyes, and I'll treasure these words forever:

"You're my granddaughter."

Yes, I ultimately lost her. As a matter of fact, I was on hold waiting for what felt like forever for her to pick up the phone at the hospital to talk when they found her, peacefully gone. Though I still fell to the floor in a million pieces, my God came over me like the eye of the storm.

And she went home to Him, just like she said she was going to.

Not long after, I clearly saw His gift in the middle of the chaotic hurt. Those moments, the time and the love. This love is a tool to

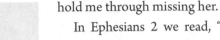

God has a calling for our lives and our hardships and will work with us to accomplish our calling. It's up to us to continue to answer it.

hold me through missing her.

In Ephesians 2 we read, "For by grace you have been saved through *faith*. And this is not your own doing; it is the *gift* of God, not a result of works, so that no one may boast. For *we are his workmanship*, created in Christ Jesus for good works, which God *prepared beforehand*, that we should walk in them" (vv. 8–10).

The emphasized parts? Soak them in, friend. Though we may never truly comprehend the "whys" behind it all and will question why such painful things happen, it is our faith and remembrance of His promises that can and will bring us through. He has a calling for our lives and our hardships and will work with us to accomplish our calling. It's up to us to continue to answer it, even when it's hard. Even in our undeniable and desperate despair, He waits—lovingly holding on to us.

This is the true beauty of His promise.

You guys, this chapter has definitely been my favorite to write, even through the tears shed. To me, it's the one that gives us the most hope as we navigate the battle of loneliness. Why? We are all dealing with our own version of a hurricane. For me it was losses. Fill in the blank with yours. And let me tell you, this isn't the space for comparing storms. Regardless of the type or size, it's *still* a storm. Some move fast and furious, ripping across our lives, and others have the power to inflict even more damage as they slowly roll across, holding us down in hurt and hardship. But no matter how or what you are going through, He's right there, loving us through it.

A CLINICAL LOOK AT GOD'S LOVE
AND OUR SPIRITUALITY

Some of you are probably wondering how I am going to infuse clinical knowledge into this chapter. Oh, don't you worry. I've had my coffee (maybe, probably, definitely too much) and I'm ready for you. Let's go!

Part of my role as a therapist and a clinician in the field of social work is to hit on all avenues or systems within a client or individual's life, especially when we start with an intake. Often, I begin with an evaluation and included is a deep look into spirituality. The biopsychosocial-*spiritual* assessment is utilized to see individuals in their totality.

You see, clinicians, researchers, and medical professionals *know* the scientific and deep value in spirituality, even if they want to shy away from it. *Spirituality is a piece of the puzzle of life and we aren't completely whole without it.*

Spirituality, in a nutshell, is a sense of delving into relationships and holding on to a higher purpose or power. Though "spirituality" can mean different things to different people, as Christians we believe that faith in Jesus Christ as the only Son of God is essential. As Paul explains:

> For with the heart one believes and is justified, and with the mouth one confesses and is saved. For the Scripture says, "Everyone who believes in him will not be put to shame." For there is no distinction between Jew and Greek; for the same Lord is Lord of all, bestowing his riches on all who call on him. For "everyone who calls on the name of the Lord will be saved." (Romans 10:10–13)

Christians have various traditions and preferences. But what matters is our shared faith in Christ.

Once upon a time, "religion" was considered a symptom of mental illness; in fact, Sigmund Freud actually connected religion with neurosis. Rude. But to be fair, there were some of what we consider today "wackadoodle" things going on back then.

However, modern psychologists recognize the undisputable power faith can have with a patient's ability to cope *through* life stressors. In fact, the Royal College of Psychiatrists in London has a designated group on Psychiatry and Spirituality. Those who go through the American College of Graduate Medical Education are required to be trained in religious and spiritual factors for mental health.[2] Numerous studies have demonstrated the positive outcomes associated with the practice of infusing spirituality or religion into your life.

The Mayo Clinic has discussed this vitalness at length and cited a survey in which 96 percent of family physicians expressed their belief that spiritual well-being was an important factor in health.[3] Evidence-based research has noted better health outcomes for patients with spiritual connections.

Think about it. When a person receives a serious diagnosis, there's typically an internal process within the five stages of grief that most human beings go through: denial, anger, bargaining, depression, and finally acceptance. One of the first questions many patients will ask at some point after receiving not-so-good news is, "Why is this happening to me?" This usually is within the depression stage, by the way.

> **God's love can and does stitch us together. Imperfectly perfect, in His way. And here's the thing—that tapestry is ever evolving.**

It's a question science cannot really answer. Sure, your physician can quote all the ways it may have occurred due to genetics or environmental factors, but this explanation doesn't *truly* answer the burning question of "*why* me?" in a satisfactory way. But as Christians, hard news should be a whole lot easier for us to process, though we're still human and will feel these same stages in one way or another.

When we are feeling broken, lost, or thoroughly overwhelmed, even the clinicians know the importance of spirituality in wellness and on quality of life. God's love can and does bind us up and stitch us together. Imperfectly perfect, in His way.

And here's the thing—that tapestry is ever evolving. Don't seek perfection but instead the beauty in all of the patches. They all tell a story that is uniquely ours and only ours. There is undeniable beauty in that.

If mainstream or what's deemed the secular society can see the benefits of holding true to spiritual beliefs, believers should feel pretty good about it too. Life stressors (our unavoidable storms) can cause what feels like unbearable hardship and devastating damage. I'm not in denial or minimizing.

I've personally witnessed the impacts of hurricanes, and though the eye or center is always calm, it doesn't stop the wind and rain from eventually breaking through. But it *does* offer a reprieve as we go through it and eventually weather it.

THE BIBLICAL ANSWER ON GOD'S LOVE

Ruth 2:8–13

Ruth's story is just brimming with God's open arms and deep abiding love! Despite obvious loss, pain, and her pagan background, she knew God's love, sought to soak it in, and believed in trusting Him.

When Boaz was told by one of the reapers who Ruth was and where she came from, she asked if she could glean and gather the sheaves after the workers were done.

To glean is to collect the leftover crops that cannot or won't be harvested. This was a common practice in those days, graciously allowing the poor and foreigners living in the land to come behind and gather what they could (see Leviticus 23:22).

Boaz doesn't tell Ruth to go away or that she was unwelcome

in his field. Instead, he not only allows her to work but implores her to stay in *his* field where he can ensure she'll be safe.

In this section we see how Boaz told the men to be on their best behavior and keep their hands to themselves, a big, big, big deal for any widow, but even more so for an assumed pagan. After his proclamation, Ruth falls to her knees, overwhelmed with his lovingkindness. She questioned why she found favor in his eyes and his response makes my heart swell.

> "All that you have done for your mother-in-law since the death of your husband has been fully told to me, and how you left your father and mother and your native land and came to a people that you did not know before. The LORD repay you for what you have done, and a full reward be given you by the LORD, the God of Israel, under whose wings you have come to take refuge!" (Ruth 2:11-12)

Ruth chose Him. She chose lovingkindness over fear. In her actions she was sinking even deeper into a refuge with God.

I think it's also sort of like the break women experience between contractions during childbirth. The refuge in those moments doesn't stop the pain completely but offers enough peace for us mamas to keep going. Even if you can numb it when you get far enough (epidurals are a gift from God, *hallelujah*), you'll still have to deal with the impact of childbirth on your body and life. Both the visible and invisible. You can't avoid the changes that come.

To me, God's love in our lives is so much like my childbirth analogy. It's peace and grace. It's also a beautiful refuge from our storms. God's love is always our safe space and refuge.

In the Old Testament, we see the word "refuge" a lot in reference to a threat, danger, or wrong. At times it's physical, and in others, spiritual or emotional. Regardless of how something is coming at us, we can always seek shelter in Him.

His love is the fortitude or strong walls we so desperately need to seek when things get hard in our storms. It's that space in our minds we go to in order to get through the hard things but also when we celebrate the big and beautiful things, like the miracle of childbirth. There is a reason He is all things. God's love is present and always ready to fill us with the strength and wonder we need to keep on keeping on.

Let's Talk about It

First John 4:7–11 says, "Beloved, let us love one another for love is from God, and whoever loves has been born of God and knows God. Anyone who does not love does not know God, because God is love. In this the love of God was made manifest among us, that God sent his only Son into the world, so that we might live through him. In this is love, not that we have loved God but that he loved us and sent his Son to be the propitiation for our sins. Beloved, if God so loved us, we also ought to love one another." In the midst of our struggles, this truth should always fill your heart. You are never too far from God's love, and Jesus made sure of it. Write out a personal prayer to seek and feel God's love in *you* as you navigate your hard days.

6

YOUR MARRIAGE
IS YOUR COVENANT

Fair warning: I'm about to get real and raw on these pages. Personally, I've been through some undeniably challenging things in my life, but nothing has tested my resolve or grit like my marriage. I'm not apologizing for these feelings, by the way. Instead, I hope I'm normalizing the difficulty in joining your life, dreams, and plans with another human's.

Add in the complications the military adds to an already taxing role, how could it *not* test you or make you want to quit?

I said "I do" in 2008 to my guy when I was only twenty-two. We'd been dating since I was nineteen, and although I thought I was prepared for marriage, I absolutely and unequivocally was *not*.

Think of it, I was barely ready to be an adult and manage myself and now I was suddenly committed to doing life with someone else.

I was the typical '80s baby, raised on Disney princess movies with happy endings and monsters slain. My vision of marriage was definitely skewed with pixie dust and perfection, but I don't think I am alone in going into matrimony with preconceived notions of how it was going to be or should be. And as a new military spouse, I had visions of grand adventures, travel, and serving this country *together*.

This was before being introduced to Murphy's Law—you know the one, if something can go wrong it will: unemployment, constantly changing plans, or slowly feeling like I didn't matter.

Friend, having a good marriage doesn't hinge on how much you "know" before you say those binding words, because no one really knows until they are in the trenches of it all. Loving and honoring your spouse doesn't mean you have to like them all the time either. There were times I *definitely* didn't like my husband and times he *definitely* didn't like me.

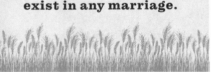

The challenges we face as a military family just add to the stressors that already exist in any marriage.

But I have always loved and valued him for what he brings to this world and to my life and our children's lives. What makes me most proud about my own marriage is, regardless of how hard our difficult seasons get, we believe they will and can heal into something even better.

We are all human beings with feelings, independent thought,

and will (thank You, God). But treating your relationship with your spouse as a covenant—which is really the backbone of the Bible, if you think about it—will be your foundation for a strong, lifelong marriage, a marriage that can weather the storms that inevitably come to us in life.

An important point: As we navigate this section, I want to be firm in addressing *any* form of aggression or domestic violence within a marriage. Verbal, mental, and physical abuse are not okay; these are unjustified and *absolutely wrong* in God's eyes—and mine. Are there times relationships experiencing these devastating abuses can be healed? Yes. But it takes *a lot* of deep work and two firmly committed people.

If you *ever* feel that your or your children's safety and well-being is at risk, seek support, please.

I like to think of a marriage like everything else in life—it has seasons. (And don't hesitate to seek counsel if you need to during one of those rough-patch seasons.)

I happen to be a diehard fan of fall. I just adore the crisp air, changing leaves, and sweater weather. But ultimately, fall leads to winter.

Both my husband and I come from what used to be termed "broken homes." We've borne witness to the devastating impacts divorce can have on children and promised to work at our marriage hard enough that it wouldn't be a viable option. There are pages in our story I wish I could erase. But without those experiences and growth, we wouldn't be who we are today.

There were times in the marriage when we had to work really

hard to keep the train on the tracks. We both made mistakes and had pieces to put back together, not just for our relationship, but within ourselves. The challenges we face as a military family just add to the stressors that already exist in any marriage. I truly feel that how you approach marriage and your partnership makes all the difference in the world.

THE CLINICAL ANSWER
FOR A HEALTHY MARRIAGE

Science cannot really tell you how to build an indestructible marriage, and therapists, like me, cannot *give* you the answer to a healthy marriage. And if someone tells you differently, pay attention to their nose to see if it grows. My comment isn't because we don't have enough research or data into the subject, but because *your* marriage is its own entity, and what works for you won't necessarily work for other couples.

In graduate school, I was taught so many theories it would probably make your head spin. We were never expected to remember them all, nor utilize each one for each person or couple we saw. Instead, our professors wanted to give us a wide breadth of knowledge to assist us in working with each individual or couple. These are the reasons why you'll see me quote and reference a multitude of people or organizations.

Clinically, we don't have *the* answer, but we do have lots of possibilities for solutions and evidence-based supports to help you figure out what *your* answers are.

Take Dr. John Gottman's research. He identified what he termed the Four Horsemen: criticism, contempt, defensiveness, and stonewalling, which predicted divorce 5.6 years after the wedding.[1] At 16.2 years into the marriage "emotional withdrawal, the absence of positive affect during conflict discussions (shared humor, affection, empathy)" predict that a couple will divorce later.[2]

He also found that the average couple waited *six years* to seek help for their marriage.

I reference him because of the extensive work he's done with marriage. Gottman has completed twelve different longitudinal studies with over three thousand couples, and some couples were followed for twenty years. The dude was able to predict divorce 90 percent of the time! So, he knows his stuff.

I want to also add that in my professional experience, many couples waited until they were drowning in hurt to seek clinical support, when in fact, counseling can and should be a part of the conversation in a marriage regardless of the season. Having an unbiased person in your corner helping you communicate and love each other better can never be a bad thing.

> **Raising your hand to get support working through something difficult is a sign of strength, not weakness.**

It's documented that those in the military community seek help for a host of mental health concerns on a much lower scale than their civilian counterparts. It's like we've been trained to, as we say in the military, embrace the suck and take hardships in stride or something (you know here I'm absolutely dripping with sarcasm).

Don't.

We are human beings with thoughts, feelings, and needs. Raising your hand to get support when working through something difficult is a sign of strength, not weakness.

When doing research on understanding what can make a healthy marriage, the Vulnerability Stress Adaptation Model is one I turn to a lot.[3] Essentially, it's a theory proposing that couples with few enduring vulnerabilities have less stressors, and those who use effective tools (that's where "adaptive" comes in, y'all) are more likely to have a higher quality or satisfaction in their marriage stability. Continuing, those with more vulnerabilities (stay with me, we'll get to what this means) and stressors and those who employ ineffective processes see a decline in their marriage—with many divorcing.

To get even deeper on this model, think about the stressors the military community encounters. There's a reason we have higher rates of divorce, substance abuse, depression, and anxiety than our civilian friends. This life is *hard*.

Also, it's important to understand that problems or cracks in the foundation don't materialize after marriage. They were always there.

Another theory I reference a lot is the social learning theory, proposed by Albert Bandura in 1977. He proved that behavior is learned from the environment we surround ourselves in through observational learning. We see this from our very first breath on this beautiful but complicated earth.

Babies aren't born knowing how to talk, walk, or to basically do anything—it is all learned behavior through observation of those around them. And people respond to behavior. As parents, we typically reward good behavior and punish negative behaviors. Both are reinforcements.

I share this to have you do some processing of your own. What was your introduction to the human relationship? Over the past twenty years or so, the clinical community has spent a lot of time researching adverse childhood experiences (ACEs). To reiterate, they are potentially traumatic events occurring between the ages of zero to seventeen.

As we said in chapter 3, according to the Centers for Disease Control, around 61 percent of adults across twenty-five states have reported experiencing at least one type of ACE.[4] These increase the risk of something called toxic stress leading to harmful impacts on decision-making, learning, or responding to stress. Those with this background have difficulty forming healthy and stable relationships. These, my friends, are vulnerabilities.

Chances are you likely walked into your marriage with an unresolved trauma. So did your service member. Without processing and learning to navigate through this, it can lead to catastrophic damage both individually and as a couple.

When I would work with couples in therapy sessions, they'd *always* look to me to solve their problems. Almost every time, that first session was filled with the hope of my being the key to "fixing" what was wrong. I always shocked them when I started those sessions telling them I wanted to get fired.

Very dramatic, I know.

My hope was they'd take the resources, tools, and education I gave and find their way. Then they no longer would need me to guide them. You can go in and out of therapy your whole life or marriage. There's no rule book on how often you will need outside help, but the goal should always be to build up your own toolbox and tackle things without constantly needing a professional coming in to help you do it.

THE BIBLICAL ANSWER TO BUILDING
YOUR MARRIAGE INTO A COVENANT

Ruth 2:14–23

Considering the word *covenant* and its implications can take your breath away. Most people accept its definition as being bound together in a solemn and binding agreement. Building your marriage into a covenant is the hope and goal.

Though Ruth is one of the shorter books in the Bible, it's packed with valuable lessons. When I read about Naomi leaving her homeland to follow her husband, I see commitment and definitely a strong covenant. She gave up her family, friends, and everything she knew without question to follow him while undertaking what I imagine must have been a dangerous journey.

She loved Elimelech even through his potential wrongdoing or poor choice of fleeing from a famine. Do we enable our spouses to become better versions of themselves, or worse ones? Love doesn't equate blindness to what's wrong. Remember this lesson as you navigate your own marriage, my friend.

When we last left the story of Ruth we were at the "meet-cute" of our budding romance. Boaz was kind and she was graciously humbled by his favor. I like to imagine her feeling butterflies and excitement from his actions and words. After a long day in the field, he invited her to dine with him. Be still my heart!

My Disney brain so desperately wants to add in all sorts of romantic touches to what that first meal was like, but we'll stick with what we have and know.

After she ate her fill, he told his men to let her glean whatever she wanted and basically to take extra. She later went home to Naomi with leftover food from the meal, plus everything she was able to glean for their household. After Ruth told her mother-in-law where she'd been and with whom, Naomi's response was to gush over his kindness and refer to Boaz as a redeemer.

It's a *really* important word to make note of.

We refer to Jesus being our Redeemer by washing away our sins. To liken Boaz to our beloved Savior gives you a pretty good insight to Naomi's opinion of his charac-

Humble yourself. Be the first person to apologize. Make it a race!

ter. If we look toward what we've gleaned (ha, see what I did there) from Ruth in developing our marriages into a covenant, there are a few key things to aim for. And guess what? They are pretty simple.

Seek grace and love even in the midst of wrongdoing. Yeah, this is a doozy, isn't it? When we're mad, we want to be and stay *really mad*. This righteousness of ours in our relationships is bananas. We treat it like a sport, if I'm being honest. Who can be the more passive-aggressive? (I always call my husband "honey," so my way is by calling him by his given name. He just knows, and it fills my soul in such a bad way.) Taking a deep breath and looking for the good even when your spouse has messed up royally is a challenge. But when you do this, much like apologizing first, the healing begins so much faster and with better results.

Humble yourself. Be the first person to apologize. Make it a race! Once you get comfortable recognizing wrongdoing and seeking forgiveness for being human and messing up, it becomes second nature.

Be loyal and faithful. These are big. Military life and life in general will bring you so much hardship without your even contributing to it. Holding steadfast in your relationship with your spouse is a surefire way to combat those challenges.

Practice lovingkindness with your spouse. Yes, this means even when they leave their junk all over the floor or do whatever it is that just drives you crazy. Now, I'm not advocating for acceptance of bad behaviors, but rather always seeking the good and the love. Remember, this was the foundation which led to "I do" in the first place.

Above all, look toward God as an anchor for your covenant with your spouse.

Let's Talk about It

Marriage. No doubt about it, it's hard stuff. I can't type that without thinking of Genesis 2:24: "Therefore a man shall leave his father and his mother and hold fast to his wife, and they shall become one flesh." How true is this? In a good healthy marriage, you should be a united force. But knowing that doesn't mean it's easy! In the previous chapter, we talked about using things that bring you joy to tackle the hard parts of life in a constructive way. While this is true for processing trauma and other struggles, this can be an excellent tool for strengthening a marriage too. Guess what—my husband and I drive each other bonkers at least twice a week. But we've found little things to reinforce our connection and "why" it's important. Coffee on the porch together every morning and walks at night. Is this a quick fix to deep-rooted issues? No, but when you are finding joy in your connection together, navigating the hard seasons is just a little bit easier. Think of some of the hardest parts in your marriage and write down some ways to infuse joy into those struggles.

7

FRIENDSHIP IS A GIFT

As a military spouse, we undeniably face unique circumstances in living our lives compared to our civilian counterparts. We've covered a lot of those challenges throughout this book. When I look back on some of the most challenging and loneliest times of my life, it was not only my faith that helped, but absolutely my closest friends who were able to be a beautiful light in the dark.

When our son Anthony was around five, Scott and I were ready to add to our family. He was finally off the ship and had received land orders for the next four years. It was perfect timing! We were ecstatically pregnant a month after we arrived at our new duty station.

I got to watch the baby's heartbeat flicker on the monitor when I was at five and a half weeks. Throughout the days leading up to that appointment, I had been filled with anxiety. I can't explain it, but I just kept feeling like something was wrong. Watching the heart beating so beautifully gave me peace, the permission to plan, and to share the big news.

Six weeks later, I saw a little spotting and rushed to the emergency room—I just knew something was wrong because I'd never once bled with Anthony. Though the medical team tried to reassure me since there wasn't any true bleeding, I demanded an ultrasound. I waited, breath held, as they moved the wand over my lower belly. When they had to switch to an internal ultrasound, I knew the baby was gone. At eleven weeks, a little baby should have been clearly visible—wiggling his or her extremities and growing. But all was still.

I had a missed miscarriage, as it's termed. Not long after I watched that heart beating those few weeks before, it stopped. My body just didn't want to let go.

I was alone in the hospital room too. Scott had already gone to work and was an hour and a half away. All I could do was cry and call my mom and best friend since childhood, Alyssa, to seek solace. The doctor who gave me the news was stone-faced, refusing to answer my questions. He left to "answer" one of them and never returned.

She hugged me tight, whispering, *Me too.* I wasn't alone.

Up until this point in my life, I'd experienced loss. My uncle who'd raised me as his own, my grandfather who was everything to me, and a maternal great-grandmother who taught me what kindness looked like. But nothing prepared me for the overwhelming grief of losing a baby I'd prayed so hard for.

I won't lie to you. In the depth of my despair, I absolutely questioned my faith in God. We'd done everything right, and my brain couldn't comprehend why He'd allow this to happen. It would be my friends who stepped forward to hold me and believe for me. In the pit of loneliness of this loss, they were the anchor I needed to make it through.

And though that doctor never returned, a nurse did. She helped me dress and hugged me tight, whispering, *Me too.* I wasn't alone. She had lost a baby and knew the misery I was feeling and processing through. We can find a friend even when we think there's none around.

Just three months later, we were pregnant again. Though I kept it a secret for some time and worried, it was completely different this time around. Not only did I find out about the pregnancy on my grandfather's birthday and the anniversary of Scott's proposal, I was pregnant but didn't know it when I'd helped the best friend I told you about deliver her baby just a week before.

And when sweet Raegan joined us on October 4, 2017, on the one-year anniversary of my miscarriage, my faith was reaffirmed. But it was my friends who sustained it for me when I needed them the most.

It isn't just me who sees the undeniable connection between friendship and tackling the pain of loneliness. Science is behind it too.

THE CLINICAL ANSWERS TO
THE IMPORTANCE OF FRIENDSHIP

Psychology Today reports that human beings with close connections (our pals) tend to be healthier, recover from certain illnesses more quickly, and they live longer.[1] Author Carlin Flora added even more to the subject by describing how friendships can be a key factor in determining our sense of self and even how our lives proceed. Her book *Friendfluence* explains how friends are, in a sense, part of shaping who we are.[2]

One of the longest running studies on friendship was created by Harvard University.[3] In the over eighty years it's been going, the results have demonstrated the vital importance of personal connections for mood boosting.

To summarize, friends make you *happier*.

Now, there are a whole host of reasons why it can be difficult to find, maintain, and grow friendships. As military spouses, the constant moving definitely impacts finding friends. For my civilian readers, life can just get in the way. But it isn't impossible, just different.

And by the way, I don't want this chapter to feel like I am preaching for you to leave your house immediately and not come back until you've found yourself some friends. The clinical research consensus may point out the benefits of friendships, but it's also clear what kind of friendships have positive impact rather than being toxic to your well-being.

The days of worrying about popularity or having a posse of people should be as dead to you as flare pants are to me—regardless of Generation Z trying to bring them back or shame me for the skinny jeans I just got used to.

To sum it up, y'all, it's about quality friendships, not quantity, because you can be horribly lonely even in a sea of people. While having friends may avoid things like isolation, true quality friendships actually prevent loneliness.

In fact, if you pop it into your internet search bar, you'll see that research indicates too many friendships can actually be overwhelming and drain your happiness. It isn't necessarily because they aren't good people but rather because you are only one person, and investing your energy into too many people can cause negative impacts to your health.

The clinical keys to deep and abiding friendships from lots of internet research (and too much coffee) indicate these are the important things to look for in building quality friendships:

Kindness (one of my favorite words)
Listening skills
The ability to be open and intimate
Trustworthiness
Championing each other

Truly, there's a whole host of things you can list out in defining what a healthy friendship looks like, but these key items are the foundation. If you close your eyes real tight, I bet you can think of at least one or two people who fit this bill. Maybe it's a family member, your spouse, or an age-old friendship that began in childhood.

Whoever they may be, their friendship truly is a gift in this world. And if you haven't found them yet, I think Ruth and Naomi might help you define what you're looking for.

THE BIBLICAL ANSWERS TO FRIENDSHIP

Ruth 3:1–5

We've journeyed with Ruth through the first half of her story. She had met Boaz and begun gleaning safely in his fields, under his watchful eye. As we begin the next portion of the romance, we find her coming home to Naomi after an eventful day—sharing not only food but the unfolding and unexpected connection she seemed to have found in Boaz.

Now, Naomi may have been Ruth's mother-in-law, but in these next moments, I think she was acting in the way a modern-day friend would, giving advice before a first date.

We've all been there. Maybe a friend encouraged us when we weren't feeling our best by making us feel special or loved, or she even reminded us of our own value when we couldn't see it. And let's be serious, she absolutely helped us pick out the best outfits and probably styled our hair too.

You see, this part of the story really demonstrates those qualities I mentioned before in building a strong foundation in friendship. After hearing of Boaz's notice, Naomi unselfishly started sharing ways or ideas for Ruth to continue to develop a deeper relationship with him. Naomi's focus was on Ruth's happiness, security, and well-being. The trust, openness, and ability to listen between these two women jumps right off the Bible's pages—at least to me it does.

Now, things get a little interesting as the chapter progresses.

In today's world we wouldn't encourage our friends to go uncover a man's feet and lie down by them to gain favor (Ruth 3:4). Truthfully, this seems like serial killer behavior to me or at the very least, a strong indication of foot fetish. And yes, I watch wayyyy too many true-crime documentaries.

But for the *time*, it was a sure way to garner notice, and in their world, a single woman wasn't a safe one. (Remember the field hands and the warning Boaz delivered to his men.) And while the episode is difficult for us to understand, what I want you to focus on is the deep and abiding friendship between Ruth and Naomi. From sticking together through loss, uncertainty, and trying to build a future, their commitment to each other's well-being is undeniable.

One verse of the Bible I feel truly resonates with the military

> **As in the military, true friends will never leave you behind and will be just as devoted as you are. We see this on display so beautifully in Ruth's story.**

community is Jesus speaking in John 15:13: "Greater love has no one than this, that someone lay down his life for his friends."

Troops will often say they fight for God and country but will almost always indicate how they do it for the person to the left and right of them too. As in the military, true friends will never leave you behind and will be just as devoted as you are.

We see this on display so beautifully in this story. I won't give away the rest of chapter 3 of Ruth, but instead I'll add in something for you to think about. Regardless of the outcome of her "date" with Boaz, Naomi was going to be by her side afterward. This kind of love is a foolproof way to combat life's hardest moments.

Yes, you will be tested, and yes, you're going to be hurt. Adam and Eve eating that forbidden fruit guaranteed us all those things, including harsh and difficult times. But when you can't hope or hold your faith through life's most unbearable moments, our true friends will do it for us.

As we discuss the blessing of this kind of connection, I want to bring us back to His Word. From the beginning God *knew* we couldn't be alone. I know He created Eve to be beside Adam to ensure there was no true loneliness. I like to imagine His hand on everyone who followed.

There have been sweet friends I've met through a series of events so unexplainable that our relationship or meeting almost seems like a miracle created by God Himself.

Or a gift.

Let's Talk about It

The friends in my inner circle are my *people* and an absolute gift from God. Think about your life as a puzzle—without certain pieces it's not complete. Our deep friendships can absolutely fuel so much good as we navigate life's stressors. I love this piece of Ecclesiastes 4:10: "For if they fall, one will lift up his fellow. But woe to him who is alone when he falls and has not another to lift him up!" Let your friends lift you. Think about your closest friendships, then take a moment to sit in gratitude for their presence in your life. In good seasons and bad, for which they aren't a fix, they're there. When I'm feeling down, I like to spend time in Psalms and I love 103:2. "Bless the LORD, O my soul, and forget not all his benefits." If we allow ourselves to go down a rabbit hole of negativity, it's so much harder to pull ourselves out. Let us rejoice in His blessings, like our friendships.

8

COMMUNITY

Life is filled with so much beauty. But I won't sugarcoat things. Our lives are also filled with gut-wrenching hardships and what can feel like endless struggle. Sinking and swimming at the same time, or shoveling rain, if you know what I mean.

We talked about needing the storm to truly appreciate the rainbow that follows. It's so true, and in my view there's no bigger rainbow than community.

Now, I'm not just talking about your neighborhood or city. The word community is so much more than a pin on a map. The *Merriam-Webster Dictionary* defines community as, among other things, a "unified body of individuals" and "a social state or condition."[1] The reason this word lights my soul up is because of the extraordinary power behind it.

A community helps build who you are, and it can absolutely change over time. My own community growing up was filled with my Italian-American family members; they were my whole world. Our get-togethers were always filled with laughing so hard your stomach hurt, too much food, and the undeniable realization that we were a unit.

There I learned the meaning of serving others, the importance of kindness, and a whole set of values that would define me and my life going forward.

Over time, it broadened to include friends and, as an adult, colleagues and advocates who believed in the same things I did. Recognizing the need for community would be one of my first lessons as a new military spouse. Without it is where I first felt the true and ugly pangs of loneliness.

Now, I'm a bit older than a lot of the super tech-savvy youth. I'm a proud "elder millennial"—a term I learned after the 56th Super Bowl half-time show. I'm not upset about it. With this title I hold comes the memory of only having thirteen television channels, a rotary phone, and yelling to my friends to come outside and play. It was the perfect foundation to ease into social media as a young adult, a whole new world.

My community is a collective group of like-minded individuals scattered across the globe. Though much has been said about the decline in mental health as a result of social media and technology, it's been the exact opposite for me.

At this stage of my life, my personal community isn't always where we are stationed. If I ran outside my new neighborhoods screaming for friends, I might meet a lot of people—including our local police and emergency medical workers. Thanks to social media, I can immediately join a local group and begin building my community without getting committed to the hospital. Winning.

We are so much stronger together, friends. And as a collective military community we can absolutely move mountains! When we talk about combating loneliness, it's impossible not to highlight the vital importance of community building.

THE CLINICAL RESEARCH ON COMMUNITY

Did you know there is such a thing as "community psychologists"? Though much can be said of individualized therapies and small groups, there's a whole world of focus on targeting entire communities for the greater good of all its members. The goal of community psychologists is to work directly with leaders within communities to create effective and viable supports for change, impact, and quality of life improvement for all.

We see this on display with community youth centers, libraries, athletic facilities, parks, and such, which feature low-cost ways of gathering together with others. Studies have demonstrated lower rates of crime, high school dropout, and substance abuse within areas of high community involvement.[2] There's power in community.

Clinically, working together for the collective good is the goal of many within the mental health field. There's a reason God commanded us to love our neighbors as the second greatest of His holy commandments (see Matthew 22:36–39). Wearing horse blinders and only focusing on your three-foot world can, most of the time, do one of two things.

One is that you could easily become much more selfishly minded, which leads to lack of empathy and grace for others. You're so focused on running your own race, you begin trampling over everyone on your path to perceived success. After a time, nothing satisfies, so you could go numb emotionally, which has consequences detrimental to your well-being. There's a whole host of mental health disorders accompanying this: post-traumatic stress disorder, schizoid personality disorder, and depression are some of them.

Another potential result of your commitment to "go at it alone" can slowly turn into a mental prison of your own making. You'll spiral so far out of control, it'll resemble getting lost in a maze without a true way out.

If I were deserted on a remote island and they told me I could bring one thing—I'd want a person. Though my first choice is my husband, if he wasn't available I'd have to choose someone else. Since my family and friends are most likely reading this book (I hope), we won't list the alternate person I'd drag with me. I love you all and you'll never know who I'd bring and that's that. Moving onward!

While I tremendously appreciate Tom Hanks's character in the 2000 movie *Cast Away* and admit freely his idea to turn a volleyball into a friend was at the very least highly creative, it *isn't* the same as having one of your people to weather the storm with you. Honestly, watching this film was like living a nightmare to me.

Though I am well aware it is just a movie, it is a visual demonstration of what is likely to occur with absolute loneliness, and it isn't pretty.

We don't realize how much ordinary interaction with people in restaurants, grocery stores, church, or just out and about impacts our overall mental health and day-to-day well-being.

The National Alliance on Mental Illness has detailed the critical importance of community on mental health, stating it creates a sense of belonging, support, and purpose: all significant factors in determining a positive quality of life.[3] If you take that statement and examine it just for a moment, you'll see the blinding truth of it immediately, I hope. Why? In the early 2020s, the world experienced a devastating pandemic that created forced quarantines for months. Even when stay-at-home orders were lifted, endless restrictions were in place as we tried to navigate this new normal.

Many people lost friends and family to this terrible sickness, and many slowly lost their ability to connect with others and feel that sense of belonging or real community. As a mental health professional, I thought I had our forced quarantine in the bag. I was so arrogant! After two weeks of homeschooling a nine-year-old, entertaining a two-year-old while managing my own workload, and completing my master's program, I was lonelier and more overwhelmed than ever.

And I looked like a hot mess while doing it. It was *awful*.

It didn't matter that I could FaceTime those I loved, or that I had my immediate family safe at home with me. My internal feelings didn't reflect that reality. Instead, I remember feeling overwhelming anxiety and despair. I felt undeniably isolated and fully alone. Truthfully, I began experiencing clinical symptoms of depression from lack of connection to my community during this time. A weight on my chest. Lack of ambition. I even began gaining weight though my eating habits hadn't changed. I struggled with sleeping well and found myself unable to manage my emotions with my family.

It. Was. The. Worst.

We don't realize how much ordinary interaction with people in restaurants, grocery stores, church, or just out and about impacts our overall mental health and day-to-day well-being. When every sense of community was stripped from me, I felt it. Deeply.

Now, I will say, we rallied as a local community and did things that truly energized me and made me feel the sense of belonging again. From kind notes in the windows to drive-by birthday celebrations, I am grateful for the people I was surrounded by. We came together through an unbelievably trying time and worked as a collective body to make it better.

That is the power of community.

I wasn't alone in feeling lonely (see what I did there). All over the world we saw an increase in mental health diagnoses as well as people needing a doctor for things like back pain and stomach upset. Our bodies manifest stress into physical symptoms and we saw it vividly on display. Throughout this time, we also saw rates of suicide increase, especially within our military community.

We have the power to change how our story goes. Own your story! Maybe you can't fight forward on your own by yourself, but you can take a step back and look around before you figure out your next move.

If you are starting to feel unattached or disconnected, reach out to your neighbors, talk to your local businesses or church, and find your community. Wherever they are. Life wasn't meant to be lived alone, and when you are struggling or experiencing a lonely season, there are people just waiting to step in and help carry you through it, just as God planned all along.

THE BIBLICAL ANSWER TO COMMUNITY

Ruth 3:1–18

In this day and age of advancing technologies, we have endless knowledge at our fingertips. The barriers to independent learning are almost nonexistent! But even with all of this readily available, we sometimes forget to look to where those answers have been all along: God's Word.

I've talked about the clinical evidence documenting the vital need for community in tackling loneliness, but our God knew it was a tool all along. As we've navigated Ruth together, we've seen proof of it woven throughout the story. Naomi followed her husband to Moab with their two sons in tow. Following their deaths, she was aching for home—for her community.

When we last left the story, Ruth was working toward gaining Boaz's notice. There were feet uncovering (Ruth 3:4) and pleas for him to spread his wings over her (v. 9). Other versions use wording like asking Boaz to spread his garment over her.[4] Now, I may giggle helplessly at the picture, but putting ourselves in that place and time, it's easy to understand why she did what she did. Without protection or a *community*, women were not safe. Boaz had already proven himself an honest and kind man in the fields, which is why Naomi encouraged Ruth to pursue him.

The idea here is Ruth (nudged by Naomi) was looking for a guardian or redeemer, which was proper according to Jewish law. A relative of Ruth's late husband had the right to marry into the family to continue the family line. And Boaz was an appealing choice!

However, there was actually a closer—relative-wise—redeemer. Boaz knew about this other man and the "rules" that were laid out. Boaz, in his worthiness, adhered to them.

After awaking the next morning, he made sure no one around would speak of her coming to the threshing floor the evening before, and he sent her home overflowing with food, saying she couldn't return to Naomi empty-handed.

We've seen the moments of value in community throughout this story. Though people may have side-eyed Naomi and Ruth when they arrived in Bethlehem, they were still welcomed. Ruth finds a way to earn food for Naomi and herself.

It begs the question, what would their story have looked like if they were fully shunned upon arrival? Put yourself there. You've just lost your husband, you were far from your family, and you'd left a home you'd built. The weight of the decision had to have been heavy, despite their clinging to each other. Had they been turned away or rejected, things could have gone a lot differently. And not just for them, either.

For, you see, I vehemently believe without the community embracing them and allowing them to feel that sense of belonging, even our lives today would be drastically different. You'll come to see why as we continue to navigate Ruth. I promise.

But know this: there's a reason your elders always harped on surrounding yourself with good people. My gram used to say, "If you lie down with dogs, you'll turn into one." At the time, I just rolled my eyes. Now that she's gone, I remember so many of her little quips I live by and find earth-shattering truth in.

Though you have the free will to do what you wish, we are influenced by those around us. And people form opinions of your character based on those you let into your circle. This isn't a dig, or a lesson on investing in others' opinions of you, but rather a hope that you'll see the truth in what your personal community brings to your life—good and bad.

After losing everything, Naomi sought refuge in her faith-filled community—it appeared she ached for it in the wake of her losses. Though I'm guessing, I feel like she ached for the familiarity, the connection, and the soul-filling feelings having a community brought. Actually, had she stayed in Moab, Ruth's and/or Orpah's families would surely have taken her in and provided for her. So it's not only for practicalities she returned to Bethlehem, but for her roots. Often when people talk about Naomi, they focus on her bitterness, but that's assuredly not the whole story. She preferred to be in Israel, in her community.

And in our times of struggle, hardship, and yes, loneliness, we too need to seek support there. Just like He always wanted.

Let's Talk about It

Planting roots can be hard when your life feels like a revolving door, but it isn't impossible. Your community can be such a strong part of your happiness, wherever you are. Let's reflect on the word "community," which traces back to the Latin word for "common."[5] What are your passions, regardless of your geographic location? Write them down! Now take five minutes to do a quick internet search and find some of those things nearby. When we feel a sense of belonging, our mental health outlook is so much better.

9

CHURCH CAN ALWAYS BE HOME

As a military spouse, I am now built pretty securely to accept change. I may whine and use choice words (that I need to repent of and ask forgiveness, if I'm being honest) with some of those Murphy's Law-induced changes, but I can adapt and overcome. While writing this chapter we are currently seventy days away from moving, and my husband still doesn't have orders. We have a home to sell, schools to pick out, and a new sanctuary to build for our family—with no current destination on the map.

Y'all, it stinks. Big time.

I may be a seasoned spouse who's used to this kind of military shenanigans, but it's still incredibly hard to manage without losing your cool. And with two children watching my reactions, I definitely have to.

Every two to three years, so many things change, and I have to pray the changes are for the good. But despite the challenge of not knowing where my next "home" is going to be or being unable to tackle the long list of to-dos for our family, church can always be a permanent home—wherever I go.

There are many churches that hold a special place in my heart.

I was raised in the Catholic Church, where I walked through my first reconciliation, communion, and confirmation. It was *a lot*. But there was beauty in so many of those memories! From receiving my first Bible (though I've discovered that the King James is *not* the best version for me) to sitting in the pews of St. Peter and Paul the Apostles, there's nothing I'd change. In those years, it was home.

Even if it was *always* the 7:30 a.m. Mass and I was *always* starving.

My views and the way I seek God have changed, so the churches I worship in have too. Most recently I was happily attending a Church of the Nazarene. But before I had even set foot inside the sanctuary for the first time, the pastor's wife had my checking account information and Social Security number.

You see, what had happened was . . . We were about to move to Illinois, and I was registering Anthony for the third grade. Well, his school refused to allow me to mail in the documents they required for his registration. Now, mind you, we'd already purchased a home specifically in the district because of the school. I. Freaked. Out.

So, off to the O'Fallon Moms Facebook group I went. I sent an SOS and received a lovely message from Stephanie Lynn, who just so happened to own a home down the street from us. I shared my predicament and she volunteered to bring everything to the school in person on registration day. She had three boys in the school herself and it was their second year.

I like to think of her as an honorary military spouse since her husband likes to move from church to church every four years or so. He shall remain nameless, since I am still peeved he took her from me.

Just kidding. Aaron, you're the best.

So, she saved me. Anthony was fully registered and accepted into the school we worked so hard to get him into! Then, she invited me to *church*. Y'all, it felt just like home should. Warm, welcoming, and so deeply loving. At that time, my husband didn't attend regularly and there were zero questions about that. Our children were brought to their classrooms for Bible study and "church" in such a beautiful way.

Now, each one of God's sanctuaries can be different. After all, pastors preach the Word differently and worship itself may look entirely different. But at its heart, "church" should be unchanging. Not only that, but church isn't really a place. "Church" is Christ's people, wherever they're meeting. It's a people. It's spiritual.

And when the pandemic took away the ability to worship in person for a time, we began watching online. And when the Lynn family moved to Florida, I continued watching Aaron preach at their new church.

Worship is a connection with the Lord, wherever you are.

As I type, I am listening to LeAnn Rimes sing "Amazing Grace." This version is sung *a cappella* and is so hauntingly beautiful. If I close my eyes, I can feel myself standing next to my grandmother— filling my heart with the same song in the Catholic Church I was brought up in. Soak in the words with me, sweet friends.[1]

Amazing grace! How sweet the sound
That saved a wretch like me
I once was lost, but now am found
Was blind, but now I see

At this point in my life, I've been in so many churches I've lost count. But no matter how different each experience was, I always felt at home. I'm found.

As I listen to this song, I am at peace. Church (and by definition, our faith in God and Jesus Christ His Son) can always be our home, especially in a battle against loneliness. *Grace will lead you home.*

THE CLINICAL ANSWERS ON CHURCH

I bet you never truly imagined seeing the words *clinical* and *church* put so close together. It's easy to imagine science and faith are always at war considering what we read in the media, but it doesn't have to be that way. Earlier in this book I talked about the importance of spirituality, or the spiritual aspect of life, to the medical and mental health professions.

The proof is in the pudding, as they say.

Christianity and healthcare have been intertwined since the early days of the church. The history of it all is pretty fascinating and is well worth looking at, but for our purposes here, I'll just direct you to this information from the Christian History Institute.[2]

But here's something: the Priory of St. Mary of Bethlehem in London was built in 1247 and was the first mental hospital in Europe, possibly even in the world. It was for "distracted individuals."[3] Honestly, do you ever feel like that description fits you?

Me, I'm distracted. All. The. Time.

But anyway, in 1547, this hospital was given to the city of London by Henry VIII, and "subsequently became infamous for the brutal ill treatment meted out to patients."[4]

Soon, the Priory of St. Mary of Bethlehem hospital was nicknamed "Bedlam," a term that came from eliding "Bethlehem," and now the word is used to describe a state of confusion or disarray. Or my house, if we are being honest. Kidding, sort of.

Okay, back to the clinical stuff. So, everything was pretty terrible for those suffering from mental illness. In 1796, William Tuke, a Quaker, had had enough and began voicing his wish for more humane methods. He promoted it as "moral treatment." He and some of his colleagues established their own asylum called York Retreat and it took off, with moral treatment making its way to the shores of America too. Eventually, it became the dominant approach.[5]

Now, there were ups and downs along the way, I won't kid you. Though many of these facilities claimed cure-inducing "treatments," they were more like experiments instead—dangerous ones at that.

I've worked in locked facilities for individuals dually diagnosed with both developmental disabilities and mental illness and I saw some horrific, shocking things only a decade ago.

Because our contemporary society has clear laws, regulations, and a culture that heavily frowns upon abuse of any kind and focuses on the collective good of a community, it was sickening to still witness such pervasive evil within those walls. But mixed in with abusers were people who had hearts of gold—caring personnel giving their all to serve those vulnerable individuals.

Let's talk about the phrase "moral obligation." What does it mean to you? Where did it come from? Honestly, this fascinates me in a way because the majority of people who believe in God recognize "morality" for its biblical roots, but it's actually a legal term, used pretty widely throughout America.

A quick internet search finds the general consensus is that it refers to what is considered right and wrong. It comes from a space of justice and equality, characteristics of an honorable person.

The phrase "moral obligation" is sprinkled throughout ethical training and obligations for a number of professions. I personally find it interesting that for a modern society so desperate to separate church and state, we sure have a whole lot of God's Word sprinkled in and through.

Anyway—I got sidetracked—the point of my rant is to point out the indisputable fact that when human beings believe in a higher power and have a connection to a community of faith or church, life is better.

With one in five American adults suffering from mental illness in any given year,[6] our profession is adamant about having all hands on deck to serve and support, especially when only half of those people receive the help they need.

The 2018 Cigna US Loneliness Index (long before the Covid-19 pandemic would worsen everything) had a devastating revelation. More than half of America feels alone.[7]

This means that half of the country feels a lack of connection and doesn't feel like they belong. Some believe that "loneliness is *the* epidemic of contemporary Western culture."[8] Now, we can attribute this to a whole host of things, especially with Generation Z (those born between 1997 and 2012) coming in with the worst numbers.[9] Technological advancements have absolutely metastasized this growing problem. The impact is undeniable. But despite this, we have all the tools we need right in front of us to make it better.

THE BIBLICAL ANSWERS
ON CHURCH THROUGH RUTH

Ruth 4:1–6

If I had any complaints about the book of Ruth, it would be that it's too short. I desperately wanted so much more detail and day-to-day happenings on those pages. Using the theme of loving-kindness in the church in combating loneliness as it relates to the book of Ruth forces us to make assumptions based on what we know from that period of time.

However, we see evidence of a "church preview" in the fourth chapter. When we last left Ruth, she was leaving Boaz and returning back home to Naomi who assured her the "matter" would be settled that day. Referring, of course, to Ruth's fate as it relates to marriage with Boaz.

After leaving the threshing floor, Boaz went to the gate to follow protocol—summoning ten men of the elders from the city and demanded they sit with him. He did what he promised and attempted to find another redeemer for Ruth, someone closer to the family, as the Jewish law required. Boaz knew of a particular individual who would have had first rights to buy the land and marry Ruth. This is what he said in Ruth 4:3–5:

> Then he said to the redeemer, "Naomi, who has come back from the country of Moab, is selling the parcel of land that belonged to our relative Elimelech. So I thought I would tell you of it and say, 'Buy it in the presence of those sitting here and in the presence of the elders of my people.' If you will redeem it, redeem it. But if you will not, tell me, that I may know, for there is no one besides you to redeem it, and I come after you." And he said, "I will redeem it." Then Boaz said, "The day you buy the field from the hand of Naomi, you also acquire Ruth the Moabite, the widow of the dead, in order to perpetuate the name of the dead in his inheritance."

Now, it definitely sticks in my craw that Ruth was lumped in with some random field Naomi's husband had owned but I'll keep quiet about it for now. Instead, let's focus on the gathering that occurred and the meaning behind the words spoken. Boaz and the men were actively working together as men of the community of faith to serve Ruth and Naomi, and to ensure they were taken care of.

Though we may find ourselves in faraway lands or lost in a sea of newness when we move, the church and its leaders should always be our home base to be closer to God. There we share a devotion to the Lord Jesus and His teachings.

The church is its own community, one that I feel deeply we can always rely on for comfort in times of loneliness. The beauty of this modern society is we can find it anywhere, even virtually when necessary.

Maybe you haven't found your church yet. That's okay! Many offer online services if you can't physically attend. Doing so could be an opportunity to find the right fit for you, though in the end you'll want to connect with a church home in person. Know that if you are struggling with loneliness, it is the one space you should always feel welcomed, included, and above all else, loved.

Let's Talk about It

Finding a church when you move often isn't usually easy. But guess what? The things that are really worth it rarely are! Deep breaths, friend. Revelation 22:16 says, "I, Jesus, have sent my angel to testify to you about these things for the churches. I am the root and the descendant of David, the bright morning star." While we can find Him in all that we do throughout our day as a guiding star, reinforcing our faith by gathering with others to worship is the icing on the cake. Write out some notes about what challenges you face when finding your church home. Then next to them, ponder the solutions to make it through any barriers to overcoming that challenge. You. Can. Do. It!

10

LOVINGKINDNESS

Kindness is my jam, y'all. Now, I don't want you to think I stroll through life like some hyped-up cheerleader for good, because I don't. I have bad days, yell at my kids when I shouldn't, say things I *definitely* shouldn't, and I absolutely get mad and think unkind things from time to time. But my internal promise to practice lovingkindness always brings me back to center.

Lovingkindness has beautiful roots in our Bible. It stems from the Hebrew word *chesed* (or *hesed*), which doesn't translate perfectly into English, but involves mercy, goodness, and steadfast love.[1] Throughout its mention we find its link to the premise of a covenant (remember that epic promise we talked about earlier) or deep commitment.

Rather than aspire to be perfect in this commitment, I home in on its meaning and try desperately to live up to this mission each day. Why? It has radically transformed my own life.

In 2019, I was blessed to be recognized as the Armed Forces Insurance Coast Guard Spouse of the Year. In a nutshell, I spearheaded food and essentials pantries for coastie families during the partial government shutdown that year, which led to my nomination and eventual award. But at its heart, it was all rooted in kindness and standing together. Though I couldn't pay people's bills or fix the very real problem of no paycheck for our service members, I *could* offer solutions to ease the burden. In my view, it's what lovingkindness can be based around.

This all occurred right before I lost my gram and was the catalyst for so much good that would take place in my story. I'd be in the pit of grief of losing her and a month later using my passion to serve others in a makeover for a Coast Guard family. In this case, the service member's spouse had been diagnosed with terminal cancer, and guess where they lived: less than an hour from my hometown.

I worked with one of my soul sisters on this project, and after it was finished, said goodbye to my gram the next day. There was much healing in these busy days and nights leading up to her memorial Mass. It prepared my heart to give her eulogy and I know it was one she'd have loved.

Later that year I worked alongside some absolutely incredible military spouses on a project we called GivingTuesdayMilitary. The mission? One million acts of kindness. Lofty, to be sure, but we were riding the high on just seeing the initial impact that rounding up our friends was creating.

You guys—those days were crazy-bananas-amazing. Yes, there were really fun things like meeting Kelly Clarkson and being on her show (I was shaking and a complete mess, by the way; I write things, not say them), but the magic was in witnessing the ripple kindness created. All over the world people were coming together to serve their communities with acts of kindness.

Pouring lovingkindness into my days radically changed my life and how I approach the things I invest my energy in. I actively seek purpose, good, and impact in all I do. Again, not perfect at it, but I'm a work in progress.

CLINICAL ANSWERS TO USING KINDNESS FOR LONELINESS

In the 1980s, the concept of a "helper's high" began to circulate. Since then, it's been proven, time and time again, to be absolutely true. When we are kind and do for others, our brains light up like Christmas trees with all the feel-good hormones that combat negative mental health symptoms and experiences, like loneliness.

Winston Churchill is credited with saying, "We make a living by what we get, but we make a life by what we give" and it's epically true. Allan Luks conducted research with over 3,000 participants who were involved in volunteering. His data demonstrated how not only did the "high" last for weeks—it returned when the participants thought about the things they did.[2]

Mind. Blown.

Being kind is so powerful you can truly breathe goodness into your brain by remembering your acts.

It's important to understand how being kind works and that it isn't just simply "feelings" but actual changes within your body's function that can actually lower stress hormones. Remember in chapter 2 we talked about the area of our brain that responds to pleasure, such as eating good food or, ahem, other enjoyable activities? It is also activated when we simply *think* about helping others, according to an Emory University study.[3]

There are many psychologists who have researched the subject and those within the social field of study have found that generous actions tend to be guided by an individual's pre-existing moral convictions. Sander van der Linden stated that "this finding . . . makes sense in light of the evidence that when people give, they experience feelings of sympathy and compassion, emotions strongly linked to moral behavior."[4] Here we go again, y'all, science and our beautiful faith intertwined like spring vines.

Think of kindness as a domino effect—it just keeps pushing forward and connecting us all in a beautiful act of good.

Now, there will be naysayers. I've certainly heard my share of them whispering about how I only do the things I do to selfishly feel good about myself. Sure, it feels good to do good, but the root of my why is never within selfishness. By living this way, I soak in the hope that I can leave this world better than when I came into it. This, too, is another lesson from my gram.

Facing negativity is another reason why it is so vital to build your circle of friendships and support well, with a strong and uncrackable foundation. It will withstand the negativity storm, which I feel sometimes stems from mindset. Maybe those who are such downers are a part of the population who somewhat disparage those considered "needy," feeling people should help themselves.

I talk about ripple impact in this book, and I believe with my whole heart and soul in its power. When you choose to practice lovingkindness with someone else, it carries on so much further than you'll ever know. Think of kindness as a domino effect—it just keeps pushing forward and connecting us all in a beautiful act of good. The sidebar fun in all of this? You'll be helping yourself at the same time.

The Mayo Clinic has published endless public data on how kindness works toward increasing things like self-esteem, empathy, and compassion while also improving your mood.[5] Remember that ugly stress hormone cortisol from the first chapter? Showing kindness reduces cortisol within our bloodstream, essentially lowering our stress. Overall health-wise, showing kindness has been proven to lower blood pressure and increase longevity. The American Psychological Association has echoed those words by adding how good it is for our own happiness and well-being.[6]

It's also important to note that all this research wasn't done on individuals doing grand acts of kindness. These are people doing things like holding doors for strangers, loving on animals, or surprising work colleagues with coffee.

For someone experiencing loneliness, especially, this can radically change their lives. Lara Aknin, PhD, an associate professor of psychology at Simon Fraser University in British Columbia, works and directs the Helping and Happiness Lab. In the *Journal of Social Psychology* she stated that "when people give in ways that are more socially connected or relational, that seems to better unlock these emotional rewards."[7] It's more than clicking a button or writing a check—you have to show up. Kindness can and is the key to all of the tools we've discussed throughout this book.

First John 3:16–18 tells us: "By this we know love, that he laid down his life for us, and we ought to lay down our lives for the brothers. But if anyone has the world's goods and sees his brother in need, yet closes his heart against him, how does God's love abide in him? Little children, let us not love in word or talk but in deed and in truth."

I love this section of 1 John. It begins with bringing so much more good news and the gospel of recognition that those of us who believe in Jesus Christ as God's Son and who put our trust in Him for our salvation are children of God. John discusses sin, of course, as it's part of the big picture, but in his first letter, we see how abiding in Jesus is the way and the truth. The message of loving each other permeates 1 John.

Lovingkindness is more than pretty words; it's deeds and truth.

Connection, friendships, God's love, creating a community, and more are all bridged together by lovingkindness at its core

And there's someone known through the echoes of time for her lovingkindness.

Our friend Ruth.

THE BIBLICAL ANSWER ON LOVINGKINDNESS
FOR TACKLING LONELINESS

Ruth 4:7–12

This story just gets better and better. When we last left Ruth, Boaz was meeting with the elders to work toward a plan for her future. The other dude he thought would choose to be her redeemer said no and in typical fashion for the time, they exchanged a flip-flop—okay, it was really a sandal—so Boaz could seal the deal on the land and on Ruth.

I just have to share what happened next, word for word from Ruth 4:9–12:

> Then Boaz said to the elders and all the people, "You are witnesses this day that I have bought from the hand of Naomi all that belonged to Elimelech and all that belonged to Chilion and to Mahlon. Also Ruth the Moabite, the widow of Mahlon, I have bought to be my wife, to perpetuate the name of the dead in his inheritance, that the name of the dead may not be cut off from among his brothers and from the gate of his native place. You are witnesses this day." Then all the people who were at the gate and the elders said, "We are witnesses. May the LORD make the woman, who is coming into your

house, like Rachel and Leah, who together built up the house of Israel. May you act worthily in Ephrathah and be renowned in Bethlehem, and may your house be like the house of Perez, whom Tamar bore to Judah, because of the offspring that the LORD will give you by this young woman."

There's so much to unpack here, y'all. We (definitely me) might be annoyed that it sounds like Ruth had to be purchased. What was actually going on was, as we've said, that the closest relative was in line to purchase the family land. If he did, he was also to marry Ruth, as Mahlon's widow, to perpetuate his family line. The closest relative we're talking about was okay with the land, but since he already had a family, he didn't want another wife.

These customs might seem strange to us—okay, they do—but I want to home in on some beautiful pieces to this part of the story. Boaz didn't *have* to marry her—in fact he was under no obligation to take care of her at all. Remember those civic responsibilities? They weren't his. Boaz actively tried to find her someone who was closer to a redeemer in his eyes, and only when that individual turned down the offer did Boaz himself step forward to be Ruth's redeemer—and keep in mind that Boaz was *her* first choice.

Now let's talk about how the elders and townsfolk responded by crediting the two women for the building of their sacred land and then praying Boaz would be worthy for Ruth, not the other way around. Around this part of the story, I started to let go of my saltiness on her "purchase."

In and throughout this exchange is lovingkindness on full display, with continued empathy and intent to serve others.

Have you ever held the door for someone when they wanted to hold it for you? It's a comical but also beautiful battle—with both people attempting to be kind, saying things like "No, you go" and "Oh no you, I absolutely insist." The smiles following are pretty contagious.

I call it the kindness dance and it is beautiful!

Everything about this meeting was filled with goodness and a complete lack of selflessness. When we strive to intertwine lovingkindness into our day-to-day, it creates some pretty amazing opportunities. In Ruth, we saw it from the beginning of her story. With everything she did, it was part of who she was and how she interacted with all she encountered.

And it's through Ruth and her lovingkindness we have our Savior, Jesus Christ. As we'll see, a pagan woman from Moab had a key part to play in the lineage of Jesus, who saved us all from sin, emptiness, and—loneliness.

Let's Talk about It

I know my overexuberant excitement on the subject of kindness can bring on eye-rolling. But I'm telling you, lovingkindness can really be the source of deep healing for the world and our own troubled hearts. Titus 3:4–5 tells us, "But when the goodness and loving kindness of God our Savior appeared, he saved us, not because of works done by us in righteousness, but according to his own mercy, by the washing of regeneration and renewal of the Holy Spirit." Even in the midst of evil, severe wrongdoing, and deep sin, our God showed us loving-kindness by sending His only Son to die *for us*. Imagine a world where everyone sought to be kind to one another. Jot down in your journal what it would look like to you.

11

NEVER ALONE

We're near the end of our journey through loneliness, my sweet friends. And journey together—we *absolutely* did! I won't lie, writing this book for you hasn't come without tears. With every step we took toward not only understanding loneliness but making it a battle we fought *together*, I've rejoiced in holding your hand through these pages.

I pray I have equipped you with new knowledge, resources, and the wholehearted realization you are never alone. You have me, and you have community, or you *will* find community. But most important, our God and His Son remain in our corners always. As Jesus said in Matthew 28:18–20:

> "All authority in heaven and on earth has been given to me. Go therefore and make disciples of all nations, baptizing them in

the name of the Father and of the Son and of the Holy Spirit, teaching them to observe all that I have commanded you. And behold, I am with you always, to the end of the age."

I am not nearly as eloquent as Jesus as recorded in Matthew—far, far from it, in fact. But throughout all the trials and tribulations I've faced, my constant was always in Him—even in doubts or heartbreaking grief. Maybe you're so far in the pit of loneliness you can't find space for seeking support or even the will to attempt to crawl out on your own.

I see you.

But so does Jesus. Though I could have started this book with this chapter, I thoroughly enjoyed the slow build and closing our path together with the most important lesson of all.

You. Are. Never. Alone.

In the empty room where you cry and hurt, there He is. Within your mind—which may be fraught with harsh thoughts and your heart heavy with their weight—our God sits, holding you up in the palm of His hands, even when you can't feel it through the pain. Know this unwavering fact; soak it into your soul.

It's easy to stay in feelings of inadequacy, negative self-worth, and the sense of not belonging, especially as a military spouse. With the constant shifts in how we live our lives, it can and does drain your energy. This constant "fight or flight" position can wreak havoc on us. I've been there.

You've walked with me through some of the biggest losses of my life and I've shared with you the ways I fought through being swallowed by them. Throughout all of it, I was blessed with loving family, friends, and access to resources to support my recovery and eventual healing. But even in the absence of those things, I always knew I had God's love and His promises.

We are all human beings and even as we strive with all our might to lead good lives, bathed in kindness and the intent to serve His will, we still mess up. Often. And in the secrecy and haunting quiet of our minds, we hold on to the shame of those missteps like a child clings to a piece of candy she wants—with strength that's simply astounding.

Guess what? Your bad choices don't need to define you. You are so much more than your worst day, friend.

Our questionable choices can lead us to feel the deepest loneliness of all. I won't use this chapter to lay out my dirty laundry, because trust me, it's always there, even if it's hidden behind all the things I used to clean and stitch up the rips. But instead of holding on to it and letting it weigh me down, I've used the things I've learned as a lesson for wisdom to do and strive for better. Because guess what?

Your bad choices don't need to define you

You are so much more than your worst day, friend. Remember, true failure can never really happen as long as you never stop trying to succeed. You are *worthy* of this life, good things happening within it, and above all, recognizing our God's love and wrapping yourself in it.

THE CLINICAL ANSWERS ON BELIEVING
IN GOD TO COMBAT LONELINESS

As we saw in earlier chapters, we have a long history of religion and healthcare correlating. We've absolutely come a long way from the times when those suffering from mental illness were horribly tortured or even burned at the stake as witches. Had I lived back then during the miscarriage I experienced, I could have been committed for my reaction as I processed the loss! Crazy times, folks. Those misconceptions thankfully are behind us, and science has navigated us toward understanding the human brain and recognizing the vitality of mental health.

Even more mind-blowing is a study conducted in which the team found that our brain cortex experiences a thickening when we engage in regular prayer, and that thickening is thought to be a protection or guard against depression, which is something often felt when lonely.[1]

Many of us have heard the adage "let go and let God" *a lot*, I'm sure. But there really is some truth in it. Whatever that thing is weighing on our minds and hearts, letting God hold it for us and guide us to the other side is an evidence-based tool for success in battling it.

Though I've already discussed the studies and data documenting the undeniable health benefits to living in faith, there's more.

Research from Dr. Harold Koenig hailing from Duke University is absolutely riveting.[2] He found through his own case studies that individuals who are "religious" or who believe in God have a strong internal sense of control.

> **Holding on to the belief in God and His hand over our lives is the ultimate answer for loneliness.**

In a nutshell, he discusses how those who pray while asking for God's guidance feel a better sense of control of their situations, which then assists with helping them cope through depression and anxiety. The era of the Covid-19 pandemic provided researchers with information about the effects of isolation. For example, in March of 2020, the world was feeling the deep grip of fear and loneliness from the pandemic. Using data from Google searches from ninety-five countries, Jeanet Bentzen reports there was an all-time high for a search of the word "prayer."[3] In fact, people reported feeling closer than ever to their faith—actively seeking God.

I could go on and on about research from that time documenting how low our world was feeling, but there was *good* stuff too. Studies from that time period show those who attended church (in any form) saw improvement in their mental health, rather than a decline as much of the population did.[4]

Holding on to the belief in God and His hand over our lives is the ultimate answer for loneliness.

The crux of it all is that when we believe God is in control and we connect with Him in prayer, when we are "going through it," we'll feel more able to cope in our thought life, emotions, and thriving in daily life. We can more effectively manage the chaos of our mind and eventually the situation we find ourselves dealing with.

This isn't a new concept. Earlier in the book, we reviewed the proven technique of thought reframing, which is utilized often in practicing Cognitive Behavior Therapy. I'm going to go ahead and call this approach our "God Shield." As you feel the negativity in your mind piling up and the physical manifestations of your stressors weighing you down, ask Him to be your blocker from all of it.

I won't kid you. It doesn't mean you are out of the fight. But with our shields, we're cloaked in protection from the dangers of our battles, aren't we? Use this knowledge to block what is harmful while steadfastly charging onward to the other side . . . with your toolbox in tow, of course.

THE BIBLICAL ANSWER IN RUTH
TO KNOWING HE IS WITH US

Ruth 4:13–22

The best part of the story of Ruth is coming right up! Get your snacky snacks and dig in, because the rest of the good news we've been waiting for is about to take place. Splendidly and romantically, I might add.

Okay, let's summarize all we've worked through. First, the story of Ruth takes us on a dramatic journey through Naomi and her family who left Israel for a pagan land, Moab, because of famine. Naomi's husband and sons eventually die, leaving her *alone* with both of their wives, her daughters-in-law. Naomi then makes the decision to go back home to Bethlehem and, though her daughters-in-law initially follow along with her, she stops and orders them to leave her *alone* on her path.

Yes, I have stressed *alone*. There's a reason for it, promise. Keep on swimming, er, I mean reading.

Ruth refuses. Quite forcefully and loudly, I might add (P.S., I really love a strong woman). This pagan Moabite clearly and confidently tells Naomi she'll go where she goes and that's that. No ifs, ands, or buts. And that Naomi's God is now her God. Y'all, she didn't even hesitate in her faith. But it gets even better!

Together, they form a bond, a covenant even, and work together to find a solution for their dire situation of being two women *alone*.

We then continue our story where we meet the charming and kind Boaz, Ruth's eventual redeemer. We read about feet uncovering and lots of sweetness throughout this portion of the book. Then, we come to our grand finale! Boaz goes out of his way to care for Ruth, shows his admiration for her strength of character, and marries her after meeting with his council of elders.

Through their union came a son.

Following his birth the women of Bethlehem blessed God for His care over Naomi:

"Blessed be the LORD, who has not left you this day without a redeemer, and may his name be renowned in Israel! He shall be to you a restorer of life and a nourisher of your old age, for your daughter-in-law who loves you, who is more to you than seven sons, has given birth to him." (Ruth 4:14–15)

They named him Obed. He was the father of Jesse who then fathered King David, and the rest, as they say, is history. Ruth, who had grown up as a pagan and a foreigner, was the great-grandmother of David, from whose direct line Jesus is born. You'll remember that Naomi was from Bethlehem, where a thousand years later or so, Jesus was born.

Mic. Drop.

It's so easy to spiral out of control with negative thoughts when things aren't going our way (a frequent experience in this life, for sure), but there is such beautiful power in our faith. I pray as you continue your life's journey, you believe with all your heart that you are worthy of being loved in your *entirety* (spots and all), seen for your uniqueness (friend, there's only one you), and above all, that you truly feel that you belong wherever you are.

I pray you use this book and Ruth's story of hardship, loss, and healing to recognize your worth in this world. There's only one you and I am so grateful you exist! Lonely hurts. But if there's anything I've learned through my own personal tribulations, there's always a new day, a new chance to work through whatever it is plaguing my heart. Take your loneliness minute by minute, hour by hour, and day by day.

Use the knowledge you've been equipped with in this book of what loneliness is, how to combat its impacts, and the beauty of Ruth's story. We are all more alike than we think and share so much in this tapestry we call living.

Even in the midst of the bleakness of Naomi's situation and choices that led her to it all, He was there. His hand was always guiding Ruth throughout her life, bringing the hope and promise of lovingkindness, of a true redeemer, and forging the greatest story ever told in Christ Jesus. Our awesome-amazing-wonderful God was always with Naomi and Ruth; they were never alone.

And neither are you, my friend.

Let's Talk about It

My sweet friend, we made it to the end. As you reflect on what you've read, I hope you hold within you more strength to navigate your challenges and a rejuvenation while soaking in the Word through our beautiful Ruth. "Where you go I will go." These words fill my soul up, y'all! Here's what I want you to reflect on as you close this book. Be filled with hope in how much you are loved!

> I rejoiced in the Lord greatly that now at length you have revived your concern for me. You were indeed concerned for me, but you had no opportunity. Not that I am speaking of being in need, for I have learned in whatever situation I am to be content. I know how to be brought low, and I know how to abound. In any and every circumstance, I have learned the secret of facing plenty and hunger, abundance and need. I can do all things through him who strengthens me. (Philippians 4:10–13)

I see you, God sees you, and even in your hardest moments, you're never alone. I promise! Write it down now. **Never. Alone.**

ACKNOWLEDGMENTS

It would take me forever to thank all the individuals who contributed to the blessing of my being able to write this book, so I'll keep it short and sweet.

To my husband, Scott, thank you for loving me and growing through this life alongside me, and for coming back for a second date even when I didn't know what the Coast Guard was. You're my greatest adventure; I love you. My sweet babies, Anthony and Raegan, thank you for inspiring me with your infectious joy for life and for giving me the ability to see the world's beauty through your eyes. You are my reason. To my family and friends, you know who you are. Without each and every one of you lifting me through my self-pitying days of doubt and cheering me on throughout my life, I wouldn't be here today. I love you.

Bianca Strzalkowski and Tessa Robinson, none of this would have been possible without you. It was your mentorship, encouragement, and kind red pen (haha) that grew me into an *actual* writer. Thank you for being such incredible friends and for believing I could do it.

To the extraordinary Megan Brown. Oh, sweet friend, how I adore you. It was you who pushed me continuously outside of my comfort zone and so much deeper into my faith. Your loud and beautiful love for God, His Son, and the Word has created a new chapter of my life that I never want to end. Thank you for believing I could, nudging me (absolutely forcefully but lovingly), and for being your wild and beautiful self. You are a gift to this world, and God blessed me the day He brought you into my life. I love you.

Gram—I wish you were here to read this and hold it in your hands. But I feel you with every breath I take, every prayer, and throughout all the good things that happen in my life. When I close my eyes to think of my life's most beautiful moments, so many of them include you. Thank you for giving me the courage, faith, and will to believe I can make a difference in this world. I love you.

To my father: thank you for always loving me, even when I wouldn't accept it. I pray you know peace.

NOTES

LET'S TALK ABOUT IT

1. "There is no reason to doubt this tradition, as the scribal/recording role of the early Jewish prophets—Samuel in particular—is attested elsewhere (1 Chron. 29:29; 1 Sam. 24:22)." Michael G. Wechsler, "Ruth," in *The Moody Bible Commentary*, ed. Michael Rydelnik and Michael Vanlaningham (Chicago: Moody Publishers, 2014), 391.

CHAPTER 1: LONELY HURTS

1. *Dumbo*, director Ben Sharpsteen et al., Walt Disney Productions, 1941.
2. Amelia Worsley, "A History of Loneliness," *The Conversation*, March 19, 2018, https://theconversation.com/a-history-of-loneliness-91542.
3. K. D. M. Snell, "Agendas for the Historical Study of Loneliness and Lone Living," *The Open Psychology Journal* 8 (2015): 61–70, https://openpsychology journal.com/contents/volumes/V8/TOPSYJ-8-61/TOPSYJ-8-61.pdf.
4. Frieda Fromm Reichmann, "Loneliness," *Psychiatry: Interpersonal and Biological Processes* 22, no. 1 (1959): 1–15, https://doi.org/10.1080/00332747.1959 .11023153.

5. Sarvada Chandra Tiwari, "Loneliness: A Disease?," *Indian Journal of Psychiatry* 55, no. 4 (October–December 2013): 320–22, https://www.ncbi.nlm.nih .gov/pmc/articles/PMC3890922/.

6. *Merriam-Webster*, s.v. "lonely (*adj.*)," https://www.merriam-webster.com/ dictionary/lonely.

7. *APA Dictionary of Psychology*, s.v. "loneliness (*n.*)," https://dictionary.apa.org/ loneliness.

8. Javier Yanguas et al., "The Complexity of Loneliness," *Acta Biomedica* 89, no. 2 (2018): 302–14, https://doi.org/10.23750%2Fabm.v89i2.7404; Suzanne Degges-White, "The 3 Types of Loneliness and How to Combat Them," *Psychology Today*, July 12, 2019, https://www.psychologytoday.com/us/blog/ lifetime-connections/201907/the-3-types-loneliness-and-how-combat-them.

9. Heather McClelland et al., "Loneliness as a Predictor of Suicidal Ideation and Behaviour: A Systematic Review and Meta-Analysis of Prospective Studies," *Journal of Affective Disorders* 274 (Sept. 1, 2020): 880–96, https://pubmed.ncbi .nlm.nih.gov/32664029/; Alexandra L. Pitman et al., "The Association of Lone-liness after Sudden Bereavement with Risk of Suicide Attempt: A Nationwide Survey of Bereaved Adults," *Social Psychiatry and Psychiatric Epidemiology* 55, no. 8 (August 2020): 1081–92, https://pubmed.ncbi.nlm.nih.gov/32683472/.

10. "Oh My Soul," track 4 on Casting Crowns, *The Very Next Thing*, Provident Label Group LLC, 2016.

CHAPTER 2: FINDING CONNECTIONS

1. *APA Dictionary of Psychology*, s.v. "homophily (*n.*)," https://dictionary.apa.org/ homophily.

2. Amy Novotney, "The Risks of Social Isolation," *American Psychological Association* 50, no. 5 (May 2019), https://www.apa.org/monitor/2019/05/ ce-corner-isolation.

3. A. H. Maslow, "A Theory of Human Motivation," *Psychological Review* 50, no. 4 (1943): 430–37, https://psycnet.apa.org/doi/10.1037/h0054346.

CHAPTER 3: GUARDING YOUR HEART

1. "Fast Facts: Preventing Adverse Childhood Experiences," Centers for Disease Control and Prevention, https://www.cdc.gov/violenceprevention/aces/

fastfact.html?CDC_AA_refVal=https%3A%2F%2Fwww.cdc.gov%2Fviolence
prevention%2Facestudy%2Ffastfact.html.

2. Todd C. Helmus et al., "Life as a Private: A Study of the Motivations and Experiences of Junior Enlisted Personnel in the U. S. Army," RAND Corporation, https://www.rand.org/pubs/research_reports/RR2252.html.

3. "Lexicon: Strong's H4755 *Mara'*," Bible Study Tools, https://www.biblestudy tools.com/lexicons/hebrew/nas/mara-2.html.

CHAPTER 4: WADING THROUGH MILITARY LIFE

1. *Lexico*, s.v. "wade (*v.*)," https://www.lexico.com/en/definition/wade.

2. "Let It Go," by Kristen Anderson-Lopez and Robert Lopez, Walt Disney Music Company, 2013.

3. "Lexicon: Strong's H2135 *zakah*," Bible Hub, https://biblehub.com/hebrew/2135.htm.

CHAPTER 5: GOD'S LOVE

1. "The Eye: The Center of the Storm," WW2010 University of Illinois, http://ww2010.atmos.uiuc.edu/(Gh)/guides/mtr/hurr/stages/cane/eye.rxml.

2. Abraham Verghese, "Spirituality and Mental Health," *Indian Journal of Psychiatry* 50, no. 4 (2008): 233–37, https://www.ncbi.nlm.nih.gov/pmc/articles/PMC2755140/.

3. M. R. Ellis et al., "Addressing Spiritual Concerns of Patients: Family Physicians' Attitudes and Practices," *National Library of Medicine* 48, no. 2 (February 1999): 105–109, https://pubmed.ncbi.nlm.nih.gov/10037540/, cited at https://www.mayoclinicproceedings.org/article/S0025-6196(11)62799-7/fulltext.

CHAPTER 6: YOUR MARRIAGE IS YOUR COVENANT

1. John Mordechai Gottman, *What Predicts Divorce? The Relationship Between Marital Processes and Marital Outcomes* (Hillsdale, NJ: Lawrence Eribaum Associates, 1994), cited at The Gottman Institute, "Marriage and Couples," https://www.gottman.com/about/research/couples/.

2. Ibid.

3. The Vulnerability Stress Adaptation Model was developed by Benjamin Karney and Thomas Bradbury in 1995, https://www.researchgate.net/figure/The-

vulnerability-stress-adaptation-model-of-marriage-Karney-Bradbury-1995_
fig5_6231234.

4. "Fast Facts: Preventing Adverse Childhood Experiences," Centers for Disease
Control and Prevention, https://www.cdc.gov/violenceprevention/aces/
fastfact.html?CDC_AA_refVal=https%3A%2F%2Fwww.cdc.gov%2Fviolence
prevention%2Facestudy%2Ffastfact.html.

CHAPTER 7: FRIENDSHIP IS A GIFT

1. Andrea Bonior, "What Does a Healthy Relationship Look Like?," *Psychology
Today*, December 28, 2018, https://www.psychologytoday.com/us/blog/
friendship-20/201812/what-does-healthy-relationship-look.

2. Carlin Flora, *Friendfluence: The Surprising Ways Friends Make Us Who We Are*
(New York: Doubleday, 2013).

3. Matthew Solan, "The Secret to Happiness? Here's Some Advice from the
Longest-Running Study on Happiness," *Harvard Health Blog*, October 5, 2017,
https://www.health.harvard.edu/blog/the-secret-to-happiness-heres-some-
advice-from-the-longest-running-study-on-happiness-2017100512543.

CHAPTER 8: COMMUNITY

1. *Merriam-Webster*, s.v. "community (*n.*)," https://www.merriam-webster.com/
dictionary/community.

2. Patrick Sharkey et al., "Community and the Crime Decline: The Causal Effect
of Local Nonprofits on Violent Crime," *American Sociological Review* 82, no. 6
(2017): 1214–40, https://doi.org/10.1177%2F0003122417736289.

3. Stephanie Gilbert, "The Importance of Community and Mental Health,"
National Alliance on Mental Illness, November 18, 2019, https://www.nami
.org/Blogs/NAMI-Blog/November-2019/The-Importance-of-Community-
and-Mental-Health.

4. A good explanation of these customs is found at "What Did It Mean to Spread
the Corner of Your Garment Over Someone?," Got Questions Ministries,
https://www.gotquestions.org/spread-corner-garment.html.

5. *Merriam-Webster*, "History and Etymology for Community," https://www
.merriam-webster.com/dictionary/community.

CHAPTER 9: CHURCH CAN ALWAYS BE HOME

1. "Amazing Grace" was written in 1772 by John Newton, a former slave trader, who experienced God's forgiveness and a new life in Christ. You can read his story at https://www.ocp.org/en-us/blog/entry/amazing-grace. The words to all the verses are well worth reading (and singing!).

2. "Christian History Timeline: Healthcare and Hospitals in the Mission of the Church," Christian History Institute, https://christianhistoryinstitute.org/magazine/article/timeline-healthcare-and-hospitals.

3. *"Christianity and Mental Health"* (February 24, 2022), *EduBirdie*. Retrieved July 9, 2022, from https://edubirdie.com/examples/christianity-and-mental-health/. The history of this institution and its influence is quite interesting; also see https://historicengland.org.uk/research/inclusive-heritage/disability-history/1050-1485/from-bethlehem-to-bedlam/.

4. *Encyclopaedia Britannica*, s.v. "Bedlam," https://www.britannica.com/topic/Bedlam.

5. Thomas Bewley, "Madness to Mental Illness. A History of the Royal College of Psychiatrists. Online archive 1, William Tuke (1732–1822)," https://www.rcpsych.ac.uk/docs/default-source/about-us/library-archives/archives/madness-to-mental-illness-online-archive/people/william-tuke-1732-1822.pdf?sfvrsn=e21108e9_6.

6. "Mental Illness," National Institute of Mental Health, updated January 2022, https://www.nimh.nih.gov/health/statistics/mental-illness.

7. "Loneliness and the Workplace," https://www.cigna.com/static/www-cigna-com/docs/cigna-2020-loneliness-factsheet.pdf.

8. Jeremy Linneman, "How Your Church Can Respond to the Loneliness Epidemic," The Gospel Coalition, August 14, 2018, https://www.thegospelcoalition.org/article/church-respond-loneliness-epidemic/. This article offers several ideas of how churches can stand in the gap of loneliness.

9. Jayne O'Donnell and Shari Rudavsky, "Young Americans Are the Loneliest, Surprising Study from Cigna Shows," USA TODAY Network, May 1, 2018, https://www.usatoday.com/story/news/politics/2018/05/01/loneliness-poor-health-reported-far-more-among-young-people-than-even-those-over-72/559961002/.

CHAPTER 10: LOVINGKINDNESS

1. Norman H. Snaith, "Loving-Kindness," in *A Theological Word Book of the Bible*, ed. Alan Richardson (New York: MacMillan, 1951), 136–37, cited in https://www.bible-researcher.com/chesed.html.
2. Allan Luks, "Helper's High," http://allanluks.com/helpers_high.
3. James Baraz and Shoshana Alexander, "The Helper's High," *Greater Good Magazine*, February 1, 2010, https://greatergood.berkeley.edu/article/item/the_helpers_high.
4. Sander van der Linden, "The Helper's High: Why It Feels So Good to Give," December 2011, https://scholar.princeton.edu/sites/default/files/slinden/files/helpershigh.pdf.
5. Steve Siegle, "The Art of Kindness," Mayo Clinic Health System, May 29, 2020, https://www.mayoclinichealthsystem.org/hometown-health/speaking-of-health/the-art-of-kindness.
6. Zara Adams, "The Case for Kindness," American Psychological Association, August 2021, https://www.apa.org/news/apa/kindness-mental-health.
7. Ibid.

CHAPTER 11: NEVER ALONE

1. David H. Rosmarin et al., "A Test of Faith in God and Treatment: The Relationship of Belief in God to Psychiatric Treatment Outcomes," *Journal of Affective Disorders* 146, no. 3 (April 25, 2013): 441–46, https://www.sciencedirect.com/science/article/abs/pii/S016503271200599X.
2. Harold G. Koenig, "Religion, Spirituality, and Health: The Research and Clinical Implications," *International Scholarly Research Notices* 2012 (December 16, 2012), https://doi.org/10.5402/2012/278730.
3. Jeanet Bentzen, "Rising Religiosity as a Global Response to COVID-19 Fear," *VOXEU*, June 9, 2020, https://voxeu.org/article/rising-religiosity-global-response-covid-19-fear.
4. CNA staff, "Only Frequent Church Attendees Avoided Downward Mental Health Trend in 2020," *Catholic News Agency*, December 11, 2020, https://www.catholicnewsagency.com/news/46871/only-frequent-church-attendees-avoided-downward-mental-health-trend-in-2020.